Contents

Introduction

The language of mathematics often confuses children and it is sometimes difficult for the teacher to explain the meaning of mathematical terms simply but accurately.

This third revised edition offers an up-to-date dictionary of maths terms used in primary and junior secondary schools. The definitions are written in simple language that children can understand, yet are clear, precise and concise. The terms are supported by hundreds of examples and illustrations.

This is essentially a dictionary for students, but I hope that teachers and parents will also find it helpful.

Judith de Klerk

a

(i) The letter A stands for area in formulas.

Example: Area of a triangle

$$A = \frac{b \times h}{2}$$

(ii) A, and other letters, are used to name points, lines, angles and corners (vertices) of polygons and solids.

Examples:

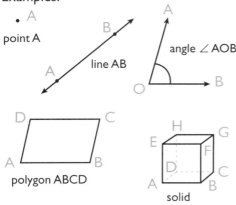

See angle name, area, formula, line, point, vertex

abacus

Usually a board with spikes or a frame with wires on which discs, beads or counters are placed. Used for counting and calculating.

Examples:

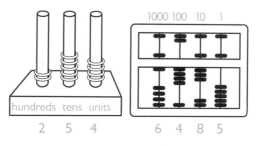

abbreviation

A shortened form of writing words and phrases.

When writing shortened forms of words we usually put full-stops after the letters.

Example:
New South Wales: N.S.W.

Note: cm (centimetre) is a symbol. We do not write full-stops after symbols:

m   cm   mm   kg   mL m^2 cm^3

See symbol

accurate

Exact, correct, right, without error.

Note: Measurements are not exact. We usually measure to the nearest unit, therefore our answers are only approximate. For example, if we say something is 30 cm long, we mean nearer to 30 cm than to either 31 cm or 29 cm.

See approximately

acute

Sharp. Sharply pointed.
(i) acute angle
A sharply pointed angle with size less than a right angle (<90°)

Example:

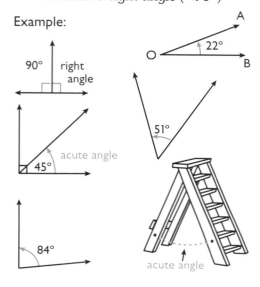

90° right angle

45° acute angle

84°

22°

51° acute angle

acute angle

See angle, right angle

(ii) acute triangle
A triangle with all three inside angles being acute.

Example:

acute triangle

See equilateral triangle, obtuse triangle, right-angled triangle, scalene triangle

AD

(Anno Domini)

Meaning: In the year of our Lord. After the birth of Christ.

Example:

The eruption of Mount Vesuvius in AD 79 destroyed Pompeii.

See BC

add

Join two or more numbers, or quantities together.

Example:

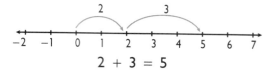

3   +   2   =   5

The apples were added together.
See addition, quantity

addend

Any number which is to be added.

2   +   6   =   8

addend   addend   sum

In 2 + 6 = 8, 2 and 6 are addends, 8 is the sum.

addition

The symbol for addition is +
(i) Joining the values of two or more numbers together.

$$3 + 7 = 10$$

(ii) On the number line.

2   3

−2   −1   0   1   2   3   4   5   6   7

$$2 + 3 = 5$$

(iii) Addition of fractions.

$$\frac{1}{4} + \frac{3}{5} = \frac{5+12}{20} = \frac{17}{20}$$

(iv) Addition of integers.

$$^+5 + {}^-7 = {}^-2$$

(v) Addition of algebraic terms.

$$2a + 3b + 5a = 7a + 3b$$

See algebraic expression, fraction, integer, number line

addition property of zero

When zero is added to any number, the sum is the same as the number.

Examples:
$$4 + 0 = 4$$
$$0 + 12 = 12$$

See sum, zero

additive inverse

When we add a number and its inverse, the answer is zero.

Example:
$$8 + {}^-8 = 0$$
$$\text{number} \quad \text{inverse}$$

See inverse, zero

adjacent

Positioned next to each other, having a common point or side.

Example:

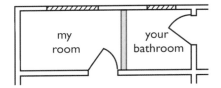

My room is adjacent to your bathroom.

(i) Adjacent sides.

In this triangle side AB is adjacent to side AC because they have a common vertex A.

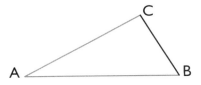

(ii) Adjacent angles.

Two angles positioned in the same plane that have a common side and a common vertex.

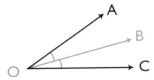

$\angle$AOB is adjacent to $\angle$BOC because they have a common ray $\overrightarrow{OB}$.

See plane, vertex

algebra

Part of mathematics that studies number systems and number properties. In algebra we use numerals, symbols or letters, called pronumerals or variables, to stand for the unknown values.

Examples:

$$🌸 + 🌸 = 2\,🌸$$
$$5 - x$$
$$a + b + c$$
$$x^2 - 2xy + y$$

See coefficient, numeral, pronumeral, symbol, variable

algorithm
(algorism)

A rule for solving a problem in a certain number of steps.
Every step is clearly described.

Example:
Use blocks to find how many 3×4 is.

Step 1   Lay down one lot of four blocks.

Step 2   Put down the second and third lots of four.

Step 3   Exchange 10 units for one ten (long).

Step 4   Write down your answer. $3 \times 4 = 12$

See Multibase Arithmetic Blocks (MAB)

align

Lay, place in a straight line.

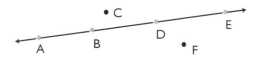

Points A, B, D and E are aligned, points C and F are not.

See line

alternate angles

See parallel lines

altitude

Height. How high something is above the surface of the earth, sea level or horizon. Altitude is the length of perpendicular height from base to vertex.

Example:

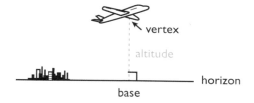

The altitude of this aeroplane is **9000** metres.

See height, perpendicular height, surface

a.m.
(ante meridiem)

The time from immediately after midnight until immediately before midday. a.m. is used only with 12-hour clock time.

Example:

It is morning.
The time is five past five.
It is 5:05 a.m.

See p.m.

---

amount

An amount of something means
how much of that thing.

Example:
The amount of money in my pocket.

---

analogue clock

A clock or a watch that has
numerals 1–12 on its face, and two
hands pointing at them to show
the time.

Example:

This clock shows twenty-five minutes
past nine in the morning.
It is 9:25 a.m.

See a.m., digital clock, p.m.

---

angle

The space between two straight
lines with a common end-point
(vertex).

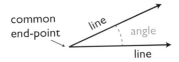

An angle is the amount of turn of
a ray about a fixed point.

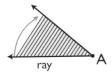

Angle is the inclination of two lines
to each other.

Angles are measured in degrees (°),
minutes (′) and seconds (″).

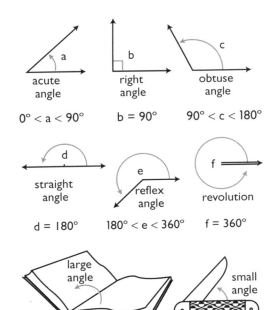

acute angle   right angle   obtuse angle

$0° < a < 90°$ $b = 90°$ $90° < c < 180°$

straight angle   reflex angle   revolution

$d = 180°$ $180° < e < 360°$ $f = 360°$

large angle   small angle

See acute angle, degree, obtuse angle,
parallel lines, ray, reflex angle, revolution,
right angle, straight angle

angle name

Angles are given names by marking them with letters.

Example:

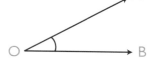

The name of this angle is <AOB. The letter O in the middle (<AOB) indicates the common end-point.

angle of depression
(of an object)

An angle formed between the horizontal line and the line of sight to an object below.

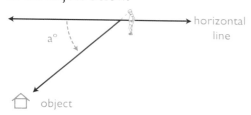

a° is the angle of depression.

See angle of elevation

angle of elevation

An angle formed between the horizontal line and the line of sight to an object above.

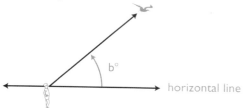

b° is the angle of elevation.

See angle of depression

angle sum

The total amount of degrees in any polygon.

(i) Angle sum of a triangle is 180°.

$$a° + b° + c° = 180°$$

(ii) Angle sum of a quadrilateral is 360°.

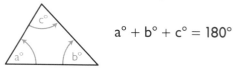

$$4 × 90° = 360°$$

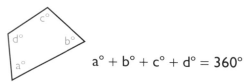

$$a° + b° + c° + d° = 360°$$

(iii) Angle sum of any polygon may be found:

number of vertices × 180° − 360°, or

(number of vertices − 2) × 180°

Examples:

triangle   (3 × 180°) − 360° = 180°
   or   (3 − 2) × 180° = 180°
pentagon   (5 − 2) × 180° = 540°
hexagon   (6 × 180°) − 360° = 720°

annual

(i) Happening only once a year.
Example: Annual flower show.

(ii) Recurring yearly.
Example: Annual rate of interest is 6.5%.

See per annum, per cent

annulus

The area between two concentric circles.

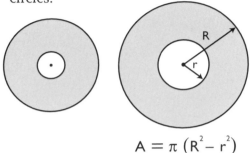

$$A = \pi \, (R^2 - r^2)$$

See area, circle, concentric circles

anti-clockwise

The direction opposite to that in which the hands of a clock travel.

Examples:

9:30

This clock is fifteen minutes fast. The hands must be moved back to show the exact time.

9:15

The hands have been moved in an anti-clockwise direction.
Screws and bottle tops are loosened in an anti-clockwise direction.

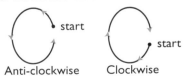

Anti-clockwise   Clockwise

See clockwise

apex

The highest point where two or more lines meet to form a corner of a figure or solid. The apex is the furthest vertical distance from the base.

Examples:

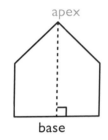

base

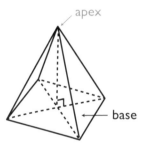

See vertex, pyramid

approximately
(Symbols: ≈ ≐ ≃)

Nearly, not exactly, but almost. The symbols ≈ or ≐ or ≃ may be used for 'is approximately equal to'.

Example:
The expressions
0.97 ≈ 1   0.97 ≐ 1   0.97 ≃ 1
all mean '0.97 is approximately equal to 1'.

See rounding, accurate

approximation
(Symbols: ≈ ≐ ≙)

A result which is nearly, not exactly, but almost accurate. One method of approximation is calculating with rounded figures.

Examples:
(i) 798 × 2.1 ≈ 800 × 2 ≈ 1600
(ii) The value of 3.14 for π is only an approximation.

See accurate, approximately, rounding

Arabic numerals

1, 2, 3, 4, 5, ... Now in common use in all western countries.

See Hindu–Arabic

arbitrary unit

Something to help us measure.

Examples:

Handspan, pace, counters, tiles, cubes, squares, bottle tops are arbitrary units.

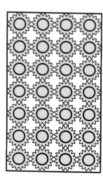

The area of this rectangle has been measured in bottle tops. The area is twenty-eight bottle tops.

See handspan

arc

A part of any curve, but most often used to mean a part of a circle.

Example:

See circle, curve

are

Unit of area in the metric system. It is the area of a square with sides measuring ten metres.

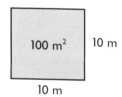

100 m² = 1 are
100 are = 1 ha

See area, hectare

area

The amount of surface or the size of a surface.
Area is measured in square units.
Units of area are:

square centimetre	cm²
square metre	m²
hectare	ha²
square kilometre	km²

Example:

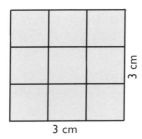

3 cm

3 cm

The area of this shape is
base × height
3 cm × 3 cm
= 9 cm²

See conservation of area, surface, unit of measurement, formula

arithmetic

The part of mathematics concerned with the study of numbers.

Arithmetic is used for computations with whole numbers, fractions and decimals. The computations include addition, subtraction, multiplication and division. Arithmetic is also used for measurement, solving word problems and working with money.

See computation

arithmetic mean

See average, mean

arithmetic progression

See progression

arm of an angle

One of the lines which make an angle.

Example:

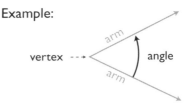

vertex

arm

arm

angle

See angle, vertex

array

Arrangement of objects, numbers, etc. in columns or rows.

Examples:

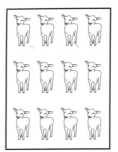

3	7	12
5	8	10
4	16	32

An array of objects in rows and columns

These numbers form an array

arrow

Used to indicate direction.

Example: weather vane

arrow diagram

A diagram using arrows to show a relation (or connection) between one thing and another.

Examples:

(i)　Relation in one set of numbers.

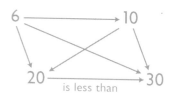

(ii)　Relation between two sets.

PETS CHILDREN HAVE

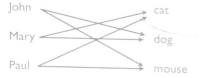

See mapping, many-to-one correspondence, one-to-one correspondence, relation, set

ascending order

Going upwards or increasing in value.

Examples:

These numbers are in ascending order:

0.1, 0.2, 0.3, 0.4, 0.5

smallest　　　　　　　　largest

These lengths have been arranged in ascending order:

5 cm, 50 cm, 5 m, 5 km, 50 km

smallest　　　　　　　　largest

See descending order, increase, order, pattern, sequence

askew

Oblique or awry.

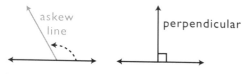

See oblique, perpendicular

associative property of addition

When adding three or more numbers together, it doesn't matter which two numbers we add first, we always get a correct answer (sum).

Example:
$$3 + 7 + 9$$
$$= (3 + 7) + 9$$
$$= \quad 10 \quad + 9 = 19$$

or

$$3 + (7 + 9)$$
$$= 3 + \quad 16 \quad = 19$$

See commutative property of addition, sum

associative property of multiplication

When multiplying three or more numbers together, it doesn't matter which two numbers we multiply first, we always get a correct answer (product).

Example:
$$3 \times 7 \times 9$$
$$= (3 \times 7) \times 9$$
$$= \quad 21 \quad \times 9$$
$$= 189$$

or

$$3 \times (7 \times 9)$$
$$= 3 \times \quad 63$$
$$= 189$$

See commutative property of multiplication, product

asterisk

A small star * used to mark a space where something is missing.

Examples:

3 * 2 = 6	* means × (multiply)
3 * 2 = 5	* means + (add)
3 * 2 = 1	* means − (subtract)
3 * 2 = 1.5	* means ÷ (divide)

asymmetry

Not having symmetry.
An object which has no line symmetry is described as asymmetrical.

Examples:
The butterfly is symmetrical.

This picture of a toy tractor is asymmetrical.

See line of symmetry, symmetry

attribute

A characteristic of an object.

Examples:
Shape, size, colour.

(i) Attributes of shape:
round, square, hexagonal ...

(ii) Attributes of size:
thick, thin, small, big ...

(iii) Attributes of colour:
black, red, yellow ...

Round and thin

Round and thick and white

Square and black

ATTRIBUTES OF CHILDREN
children with

Other classifications different from the examples above are clearly possible.

See classify, property

average

The average of a collection of numbers or scores is one score which represents the whole collection. It is found by adding all of the scores and dividing the answer (sum) by the number of scores.

Example:
Find the average of scores 2, 5, 4, 6 and 3.

$$\text{Average} \quad = \quad \frac{\text{sum of scores}}{\text{number of scores}}$$

$$= \quad \frac{2 + 5 + 4 + 6 + 3}{5}$$

$$= \quad \frac{20}{5}$$

Average = 4

This is also called the **mean** or **arithmetic mean**.

See mean, score, sum

axis

(Plural: axes)

(i) The lines which form the
framework for a graph. The
horizontal axis is called x-axis,
the vertical axis is called
y-axis. Both axes are marked
with equally spaced scales. The
point where the axes intersect
is called the origin (O).

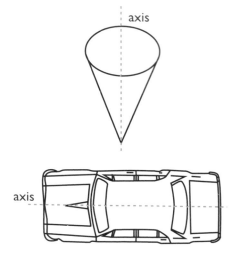
axis

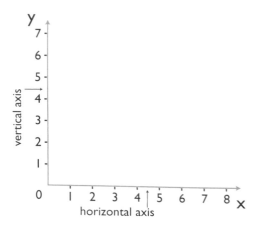

See coordinates, graph, horizontal,
intersection, line of symmetry, origin,
vertical

Axes are sometimes called:
x-axis = abscissa
y-axis = ordinate

(ii) A main line going through the
centre of a figure or solid, also
called a line of symmetry.

Examples:

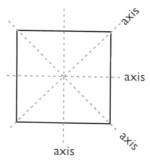

axis of symmetry

See line of symmetry

bar graph

A graph which uses horizontal or vertical bars to represent various kinds of information. A bar graph with vertical bars or columns is also called a column graph.

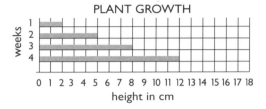

PLANT GROWTH

weeks

height in cm

CARS SOLD IN MAY

See column graph, graph, pie graph, pictograph

balance

(i)   An equal distribution.

balanced   unbalanced

(ii) Balance scales is a name given to some kinds of scales used for weighing things.

Example:

a spring balance

(iii) The amount of money in a bank account.

Date	Description	Credit	Debit	Balance
2001				
02 Feb	Pay	350		
05 Feb	ATM withdrawal		200	150
10 Feb	Rent		50	100
16 Feb	Pay	350		450
21 Feb	Rates		295	155

base

(i)   The face on which a shape or a solid stands.

Examples:

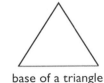

base of a triangle

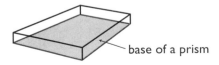

base of a prism

(ii) The number on which a place value system of numeration is constructed.

Example:

The Hindu–Arabic system is a base 10 system.

hundreds	tens	units	tenths

10× bigger

100× bigger

10× smaller

(iii) A number, symbol or a variable used with index to show an index notation.

Examples:

index

2^3 a^4 x^a

base

In index notation, the base is the number we read first.
In 2^3, read 'two cubed', 2 is called the base.

See decimal place-value system, exponent, index, index notation, power of a number

....

base line

(i) The horizontal axis of a graph.

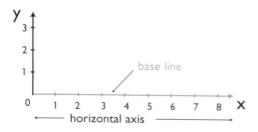

base line

horizontal axis

(ii) A base from which the heights of objects may be compared.

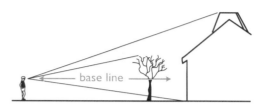

base line

See axis, horizontal line

....

base ten system

See decimal place-value system, decimal system, index, index notation, power of a number

....

basic facts

Operations performed with one-digit numbers 0, 1, 2, 3, 4, 5, 6, 7, 8 and 9.

Examples:

Addition
$0 + 0 = 0$ $0 + 1 = 1$
$1 + 1 = 2$ $9 + 9 = 18$

Subtraction corresponds with addition.

Multiplication
$0 \times 0 = 0$ $0 \times 1 = 0$
$1 \times 1 = 1$ $9 \times 9 = 81$

Division corresponds with multiplication.

(Note: It is not possible to divide by zero!)

See digit, operation, zero

battleships

A game in which two players have identical grids on which they mark in 'battleships' in random positions. Each has to guess the position of the opponent's battleships by naming either:

(i) the cells on the grid

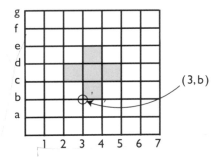

(D,3)

or

(ii) points of intersection of lines to pin-point their location

(3,b)

(Note: Ordered pairs are used to locate the cells or the points.)

See coordinates, grid, ordered pair, random

beam balance

Any balance where a beam is used.

Examples:

a seesaw   a beam balance

A beam balance is used to measure the mass of an object by balancing it with an object whose mass is known.

See balance, mass

bearing

A horizontal angle measured from 0° to 90° between a north or south direction and the direction of the object.

True bearings are measured to the true north direction, magnetic bearings to the magnetic north (or south).

Example:

bearing is N 35° E

35°

See compass, direction

BC
(Before Christ)

The years before Christ was born.

Example: Egyptian Pharaoh Tutankhamen ruled in 14th century BC.

See AD

bicentenary

200th anniversary.

Example:

1970 marked the bicentenary of Captain Cook's landing at Botany Bay.

billion

A billion is understood to be one thousand millions.

1 000 000 000 or (10^9)

Note: A billion used to be a million millions.

binary

A base-2 number system that uses only 0 and 1 to represent numbers. It is the smallest number system used to represent information. All numbers can be represented in a binary system.

Example:

Binary (Base-2) system.

Place value	a^7	a^6	a^5	a^4	a^3	a^2	a^1	a^0	
Binary	2^7	2^6	2^5	2^4	2^3	2^2	2^1	2^0	
Value	128	64	32	16	8	4	2	1	Number
								0	0
							0	1	1
							1	0	2
						0	1	1	3
						1	0	0	4
				0	1	0	1	0	10
				0	1	1	1	1	15
			0	1	1	0	0	1	25
	1	0	0	0	1	1	0	0	140

binomial

In algebra, an expression consisting of two terms joined by + or −. The terms are called monomials.

Examples:

$2 + a$ $3a - b$ $2x^2 + y^2$

See algebra

bisect

To cut or divide into two equal parts.

This angle has been bisected.

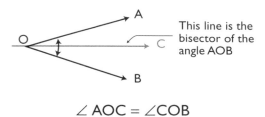

This line is the bisector of the angle AOB

$\angle AOC = \angle COB$

bisector

A straight line which divides an angle, or an interval, into two equal parts.

Examples:

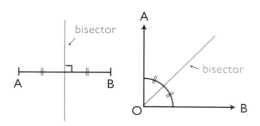

bisector

See bisect, interval, midpoint

boundary

A line around the edge of a region.

Examples:

(i) The boundary around a soccer field.

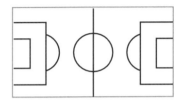

(ii) The boundary of Queensland.

(iii) A boundary of a hexagon is its perimeter.

See perimeter, region

brackets

The signs $(\ )\ [\ ]\ \{\ \}$ are used for grouping things or numbers together.

ordinary brackets   square   braces
(parentheses)   brackets

Brackets are used to indicate the order of operations.

Example:

$$5\{2\,[4(3+10)-(35\div5)-8]\}$$

$= 5\{2\,[(4\times13)-7-8]\}$ ① remove ordinary brackets

$= 5\{2\,[52-15]\}$ ② remove square brackets

$= 5\{2\times37\}$ ③ remove braces

$= 5\times74 = 370$

See grouping symbols, order of operations

breadth

Measurement from side to side, also called 'width'.

Example:

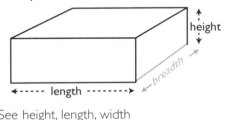

See height, length, width

budget

A plan for using money.

Example:

Jessica earns $196 a fortnight. Her budget is:

Board and food	$60
Bus fares	$16
Clothes	$25
Entertainment	$30
Savings	$65
Total	$196

C

(i) C is a symbol for Celsius
     temperature scale.

     0°C   water freezes

     100°C   water boils

(ii) A symbol for circumference in
     formulas.

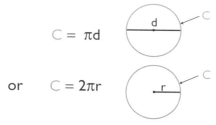

     $C = \pi d$

or $C = 2\pi r$

(iii) In Roman numerals, C stands
      for one hundred.

      $CCCXXII = 322$

calculate

Work out the answer. Using
mathematical procedures to
determine a number, quantity or
expression.

calculator

Calculating aid.
Calculators are
electronic. They are
battery or solar
powered.

calendar

A calendar represents the way in
which a year is broken up into
months, weeks and days.

Example:

2000

January
M T W T F S S
31   1 2
3 4 5 6 7 8 9
10 11 12 13 14 15 16
17 18 19 20 21 22 23
24 25 26 27 28 29 30

The third Tuesday
in February 2000
is the 15th.

See day, leap year,
month, year

February
M T W T F S S
1 2 3 4 5 6
7 8 9 10 11 12 13
14 (15) 16 17 18 19 20
21 22 23 24 25 26 27
28 29

calliper

A measuring instrument similar to
compasses with curved legs for
measuring thickness (diameter) of
curved (convex) objects or, turned
outwards, for measuring cavities.

thickness

size
of cavity

See compasses, concave, convex

cancelling

A method of changing a fraction to its simplest form.

Examples:

(i) Divide both numerator and denominator by three (common factor).

$$\frac{15^{\div 3}}{21_{\div 3}} = \frac{\cancel{15}^{\,5}}{\cancel{21}_{\,7}} = \frac{5}{7}$$

(ii) Divide across.

$$\frac{^{3}\cancel{15}}{_{2}\cancel{22}} \times \frac{\cancel{33}^{\,3}}{\cancel{40}_{\,8}} = \frac{3 \times 3}{2 \times 8} = \frac{9}{16}$$

See denominator, fraction, numerator, simple fraction, simplify

capacity

How much a container can hold. The number of cubic units a container can hold is called the capacity or volume of the container. Volume is the actual amount of material in the container.
Units of capacity are:

cubic centimetre	cm^3
cubic metre	m^3
millilitre	mL
litre	L
kilolitre	kL
megalitre	ML
1 mL	$= 1\ cm^3$
1000 mL	$= 1\ L = 1000\ cm^3$
1000 L	$= 1\ kL = 1\ m^3$

Example:
An eye dropper holds about 1 millilitre of liquid, which fills one cubic centimetre.

See volume, metric relationships on page 151

cardinal number

The number of all elements (members) in a set. When we count, we give each element one number, starting with 1. These numbers are in sequence. The last number given is the cardinal number of the set.

Example:
How many balloons?

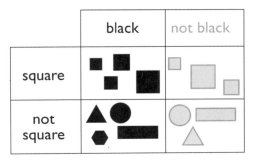

The cardinal number of this set of balloons is 5.

See counting, sequence, set

Carroll diagram

A method of recording a classification activity (used by Lewis Carroll).

	black	not black
square		
not square		

See attribute, classify, diagram sorting

carrying

Another word for regrouping.

Example:

$$\begin{array}{r} 25 \\ +\ 1\llap{,}8 \\ \hline 33 \end{array}$$

Add 5 + 8 = 13
write 3 in unit column
and carry 1 into tens
column

See regroup

Cartesian coordinates

See coordinates

cc

A symbol sometimes used to show cubic centimetre. The correct symbol is cm³.

See cubic centimetre

Celsius scale

See C, degree Celsius, temperature

cent

(Symbol: c)

One cent is one hundredth of a dollar.

1c = $0.01

$1 = 100c

One cent used to be the smallest coin in Australian currency. Now it is the five cent coin.

See dollar

Centigrade

Old name used for a temperature scale divided into 100 degrees. We now call it the Celsius scale.

See degree Celsius, temperature

centimetre

(Symbol: cm)

A unit of length.

1 cm = 0.01 m

1 cm

100 cm = 1 m

Example:

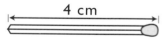

4 cm

This match is four centimetres long.

See length, unit of measurement

centre

A point that is the same distance from all points of a circle, a sphere, etc.

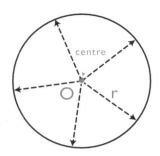

The distance is called radius (r).

See circle, circumference, radius

century

One hundred.

Examples:
100 years, 100 runs in cricket, etc.

From 1 January 1901 to 31 December 2000 is the 20th century.

The 21st century begins on 1 January 2001.

chance

A likelihood of an event happening.

See probability

chance event

An event of which the outcome is uncertain.

For some events we can predict a possible outcome, but we can never be sure.

Examples:
Tossing a coin, rolling a die, drawing a coloured marble from a bag.

See probability

checking

A way of making sure that an answer is correct. One way of checking is by using the inverse operation.

Examples:

(i) Addition is checked by subtraction.

$$\begin{array}{r} 15 \\ +\ 28 \\ \hline 43 \end{array} \qquad \begin{array}{r} 43 \\ -\ 28 \\ \hline 15 \end{array}$$

The answer **43** is correct.

(ii) Division is checked by multiplication.

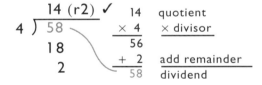

The answer **14 (r2)** is correct.

See inverse, inverse operation

chord

A line joining two points on a circle.

Examples:

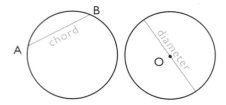

The diameter is the longest chord in a circle.

See circumference, diameter

chronological order

Events arranged by the date or time when they happened.

Example: The history of π

Time	Who/Where	Value of π
2000 BC	Babylonia	$3\frac{1}{8}$
300 BC	Archimedes	$3\frac{10}{71}$ to $3\frac{1}{7}$
1220 AD	Fibonacci	3.141 818
1665	Newton	3.141 592 653 589 7932
1705		π sign was first used
1949	ENIAC computer	π correct to 2035 decimal places
1984	Tokyo	π computed to 16 million decimal places

See pi, time line

circle

The set of all points in a plane which are at the same distance (radius r) from a given point O (centre).

Example:

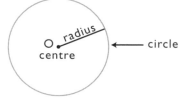

See centre, circumference, diameter, plane, radius of a circle

circle graph

See pie graph

circumference

The perimeter of a circle. The distance around a circle.

If the radius is r units, then the circumference C is $2\pi r$ units.

$$C = 2\pi r$$

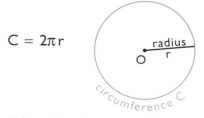

When the diameter d is measured, then the circumference C is πd units.

$$C = \pi d$$

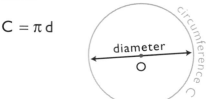

See circle, diameter, perimeter, pi (π)

class

A group, set, or a collection of things.

Example:

Triangles, squares, rectangles and kites belong to the class of polygons.

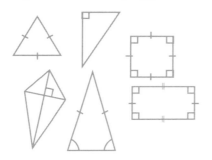

See classification, classify, collection

classification

Arrangement into classes, sets or groups, according to attributes.

Examples:

	not purple	purple
△	△ ▽ ◣ ◿ ◣	◣ ◢ ◿
not △	⊘ ▨ ⊘	● ◼ ▬

Have pets	Don't have pets
Quong	Halima
Kelly	Nick
Grant	Dean
Toula	Anna
Ali	Scott
Claire	Sachiko

See attribute, property

classify

Sort objects, ideas or events into groups, classes or hierarchies according to one or more properties or attributes.

See attribute, property, sorting

clockwise

The direction in which the hands of a clock normally travel.

Example:

start

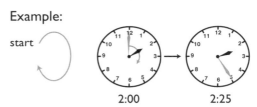

2:00   2:25

The hands on this clock have moved in a clockwise direction.

Screws and bottle tops are tightened clockwise.

See anticlockwise

closed curve

A curve which starts at a point and comes back to that point.

Examples:

(i)   simple closed curves

(ii) closed curves that are not simple

(iii) regular closed curves

See circle, curve, ellipse, open curve

closed shape

A shape (polygon) whose sides begin and end at the same point.

Examples:

closed shapes

These are not closed shapes.

See polygon, shape

cm

A symbol for centimetre.

See centimetre, symbol

code

A system of words, letters or symbols which represent other letters, words or sentences. Codes are used for secret writing or signalling.

Example: Morse code

coefficient

The number (constant term) in front of a pronumeral (variable) in an algebraic term.

Examples:

3y	3 is the coefficient of y
7(a+b)	7 is the coefficient of (a+b)
xy	coefficient is 1

See algebra, pronumeral

cointerior angles

See parallel lines

collinear

Three or more points that lie on the same straight line.

A, B, C and D are collinear points

See line, point

column

A vertical arrangement.

Examples:

13
5
18
27
9

column of numbers   column of cars

See column graph

column graph

A graph that uses columns of different lengths to represent various kinds of information.

Example:

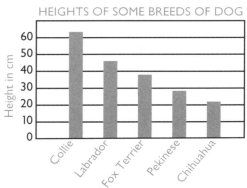

HEIGHTS OF SOME BREEDS OF DOG

See bar graph, column

combination

A subgroup of a given group.

Example:

There are four shapes in this group.

The possible pairings are:

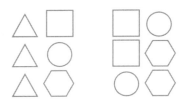

Each pairing is called a **combination**.

The order in which the shapes are placed is not important.

See permutation, set, subset

combined shapes

(complex)

Plane shapes that are made of two or more polygons.

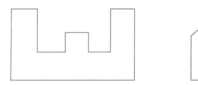

To calculate the area of a combined shape, divide it into simple shapes.

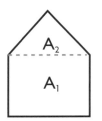

$$\text{Area} = A_1 + A_2$$

common denominator

For two or more fractions, a common denominator is a number into which all the denominators divide exactly.

Example:

For the fractions $\frac{1}{2}$ and $\frac{1}{3}$ a common denominator is 6, and also 12, 18, 24, etc.

6 is the lowest common denominator (LCD).

See denominator, fraction, lowest common denominator

common fraction

See simple fraction

commutative property of addition

The order in which two or more numbers are added does not affect the answer (sum).

Example:

6 + 4 = 4 + 6

   10 = 10

See associative property of addition, sum

commutative property of multiplication

The order in which two or more numbers are multiplied does not affect the answer (product).

Example:

$3 \times 8 = 8 \times 3$

   24 = 24

See associative property of multiplication, product

comparison

Identifying whether objects, measures or quantities are the same or different.

Examples:

same objects   different objects

same heights   different heights

See division, ratio

compass

An instrument which shows direction. Used in ships, aeroplanes, etc.

Example:

See bearing, direction

compasses
(pair of)

An instrument used to draw a circle and to mark off equal lengths. Often called a compass, for short.

complement

Something that completes or fills up a whole.

See complementary addition, complementary angles

complementary addition

(i) Finding the amount to complete a set.

Example:

What has to be added to seven to make ten?

$7 + \square = 10$

$7 + 3 \quad = 10$

Answer: Three has to be added.

(ii) Counting on to a higher total (as change is given after a purchase).

Example:

Shopping costs $17.50. I pay with a $20 note. I get $2.50 change. This is evaluated by finding what must be added to $17.50 to make $20.

(iii) The method of 'subtracting' which converts the subtraction question to an addition question.

Example:

$21 - 19 = 2$

Instead of taking nineteen away from twenty-one we think how much must be added to nineteen to make twenty-one.

See addition, set, subtraction

complementary angles

Two angles that together make 90°.

Example:

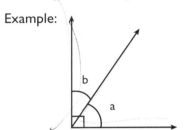

$a + b = 90°$

$\angle a$ and $\angle b$ are complementary.

$\angle a$ is the complement of $\angle b$.

$\angle b$ is the complement of $\angle a$.

See supplementary angles

complex fraction

A fraction whose numerator, denominator, or both, are fractions.

Examples:

$$\frac{\frac{1}{2}}{5} \qquad \frac{3}{\frac{4}{7}} \qquad \frac{\frac{1}{2}}{\frac{3}{4}} \qquad \frac{\frac{a}{b}}{\frac{c}{d}}$$

Note: To simplify a complex fraction means the same as division of fractions. It can be done in two ways:

Divide $\frac{1}{2}$ by $\frac{2}{3}$.

1. $\quad \frac{1}{2} \div \frac{2}{3} = \frac{1}{2} \times \frac{3}{2} = \frac{3}{4}$

2. $\quad \left(\dfrac{\frac{1}{2}}{\frac{2}{3}} \right) = \frac{1 \times 3}{2 \times 2} = \frac{3}{4}$

composite number

A number with factors other than itself and one.

Examples:

12 = 12 × 1 = 3 × 4 = 3 × 2 × 2

33 = 33 × 1 = 3 × 11

Both twelve and thirty-three are composite numbers.

17 = 17 × 1   23 = 23 × 1

Seventeen and twenty-three are not composite numbers.

Numbers like seventeen which have no other factors except themselves and one are called prime numbers.

Every whole number greater than one is either:

(i)   a prime number
      (2, 3, 5, 7, 11 ...)
or
(ii) a composite number
      (4, 6, 8, 9, 10, 12, 14 ...)

See factors, prime number

compound operation

See order of operations

computation

Using addition, subtraction, multiplication and/or division to find the answer. These operations can be performed mentally, in writing or with the help of calculating aids such as an abacus, tables, calculators or computers.

See abacus, calculator, computer, table

compute

To work out or calculate.

Example:

$$
\begin{array}{r}
^14.7 \\
\times\,^23.21 \\
\hline
47 \\
940 \\
14100 \\
\hline
15.087
\end{array}
$$

concave

A shape that is hollowed or rounded inward like the inside of a bowl.

Examples:

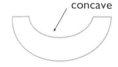

concave

concave lens

See convex

concentric circles

Circles that are in the same plane and have the same centre are concentric.

Example:

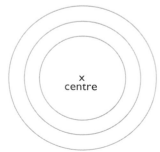

x centre

See annulus, circle, plane

concurrent lines

Lines that intersect at the same point.

See intersect, parallel lines

cone

A solid which has a circular base and comes in to a point at the top, similar in shape to an ice-cream cone.

Examples:

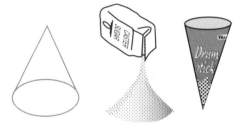

See right 3D shape, solid

congruent

(Symbol: ≡)

Exactly equal. Matching exactly. Two figures are congruent if they have the same shape and the same size.

Examples:

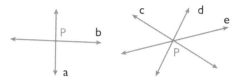

Circle A is congruent to circle B.

A ≡ B

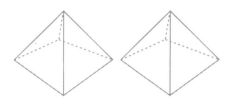

Congruent pyramids

See corresponding angles, similar

conic section

A figure (ellipse, parabola, or hyperbola) formed when a right circular cone is cut by a plane.

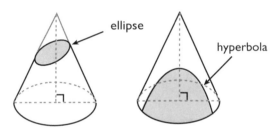

See ellipse

consecutive numbers

Numbers that follow each other in a sequence.

Examples:

$$1\ 2\ 3\ 4\ 5\ 6\ 7\ 8 \ \ldots$$

$$\frac{1}{7}\ \frac{2}{7}\ \frac{3}{7}\ \frac{4}{7}\ \frac{5}{7}\ \frac{6}{7} \ \ldots$$

$$0.1\ \ 0.2\ \ 0.3\ \ 0.4 \ \ldots$$

See sequence

conservation of area

Retaining the same area.

Examples:

(i) The three triangles have the same area
$A = \frac{1}{2} \times 2 \text{ cm} \times 2.5 \text{ cm} = 2.5 \text{ cm}^2$,
even though their shapes are different.

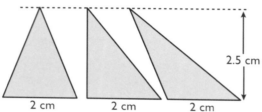

2 cm　　　2 cm　　　2 cm

2.5 cm

(ii) The three shapes have the same area of 3 cm².

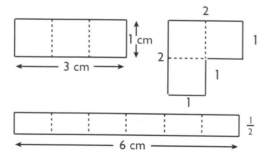

See area

constant

A number that always has the same value.

Example:

$2c + 6$

6 is the constant.

converging lines

Two or more lines that meet at the same point.

P

See perspective

convex

Shaped like the outside of a circle or a sphere. The opposite of concave.

convex lens

See concave, irregular, regular

coordinates

A pair of numbers or letters that show the position of a point on the plane. The first number is always the x-coordinate, the second is the y-coordinate.

Examples:

(i) Each point on the plane is given an ordered pair of numbers, written in parentheses.

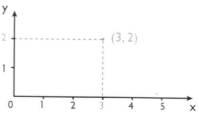

Point (3, 2) has the x-coordinate 3, and the y-coordinate 2.

(ii) The position of Laura Street is D3.

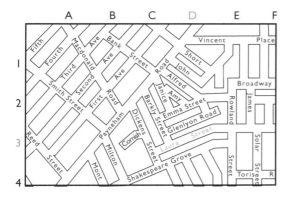

See axis, intersection, ordered pair, origin

coplanar

Lying or being in the same plane.

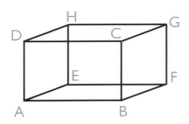

C, D, G and H are coplanar points. AB and CG are not coplanar.

correspondence

See one-to-one correspondence, many-to-one correspondence

corresponding angles

Angles in the same or similar position. In congruent shapes, corresponding angles have the same size (are congruent).

Example:

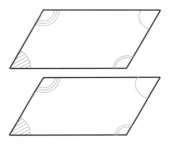

These parallelograms are congruent. Corresponding angles are marked by the same symbol.

See congruent, parallel lines, vertically opposite

corresponding sides

In congruent shapes, like the triangles below, the sides AB and XY, BC and YZ, and CA and ZX are corresponding sides.

Example:

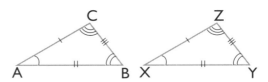

See congruent

cost

The price of something.

counting

Giving one number to every item in a set. These numbers are in a sequence.

Example:

The numbers 1, 2, 3, 4, 5 ... are counting numbers.

See cardinal number, sequence, set

counting number

A member of the set of numbers used in counting: {1, 2, 3, 4 ...} Note: zero is not a counting number.

See cardinal number, number

counting system

A way of finding out how many objects there are.

See decimal place-value system

cross-section of a solid

The face that is made when a solid is cut through by a plane.

Example:

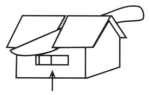

If you cut a house in half like this,

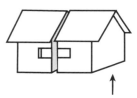

and took away this half,

then looking from here,

you would see this cross-section.

See face, front view, plan, plane, side view

cube

A solid, shaped like a box, with twelve equal edges, six equal square faces and eight corners. A cube is a type of cuboid.

Examples:

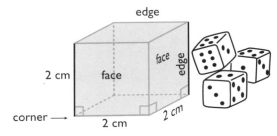

This is a diagram of a 2 cm cube.

See cuboid, face, solid

cubed number

4^3 means $4 \times 4 \times 4$ or 64.
We read it as '4 cubed', '4 cube' or '4 to the third power'.

See index, index notation, power of a number, square number

cubic centimetre

(Symbol: cm^3)

A cubic centimetre is a unit for measuring volume.

Example:

It is a cube with edges of 1 cm.

$1 \ cm^3$ has a capacity of 1 millilitre.

See capacity, cube, unit of measurement, volume

cubic metre

(Symbol: m^3)

A cubic metre is a unit for measuring volume.

Example:

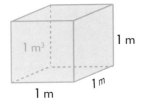

A cube whose edges are 1 metre long has a volume of 1 cubic metre.

$1 \ m^3 = 1 \ 000 \ 000 \ cm^3$

$1 \ m^3$ has a capacity of 1 kilolitre.

See capacity, unit of measurement, volume

cubic unit

A measure of volume.

See cubic centimetre, cubic metre, volume

cuboid

A shape such as a shoe box. A cube-like prism. It has twelve edges, six faces and eight corners. The opposite faces are the same shape and size.

Examples:

These packets are cuboids.

See cube, face, prism

curve

A line of which no part is straight. There are open curves and closed curves.

Examples:

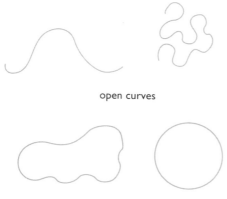

open curves

closed curves

See closed curve, open curve

cycle

A system that repeats itself in time.

Example:

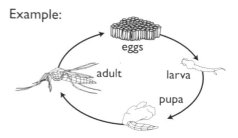

The breeding cycle of mosquitoes.

cycle game

A game that follows a set of rules in which the last move returns the player to the starting point.

Examples:

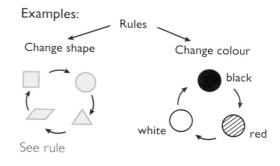

See rule

cylinder

A cylinder is a shape like a can. It is a solid with two circular faces at right angles to a curved surface.

Examples:

See capacity, graduated, right 3D shape

data

A general term used to describe a collection of facts, numbers, measurements or symbols.

Example:

Students' scores in a maths test were 15, 16, 18, 19, 19, 20, 21, 21, 22 marks.

date

Specified time: day, month or year, at which something takes place.

Example:

The date on my letter is 10 May 1998.

day

The 24-hour period it takes the earth to turn once on its axis.

days of the week

Weekdays are: Monday, Tuesday, Wednesday, Thursday and Friday. Weekend days are: Saturday and Sunday.

decade

Ten years.

decagon

A polygon with ten sides.

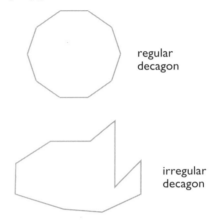

regular decagon

irregular decagon

See polygon

decahedron

A polyhedron with ten faces.

Example:

This decahedron has been made by joining two pyramids and cutting their tops off.

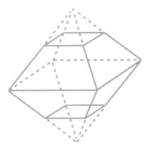

See frustum, polyhedron

decimal

Containing ten parts.

decimal fraction

A fraction written as a decimal.

Example:

$$\frac{1}{10} = 0.1$$

simple   decimal
fraction   fraction

See decimal place-value system

decimal place-value system

A numeration system with ten as a base for grouping. Commonly called the 'base ten' system.

10^6 10^5 10^4 10^3 10^2 10^1 10^0 10^{-1} 10^{-2} 10^{-3}

millions	hundred thousands	ten thousands	thousands	hundreds	tens	units	tenths	hundredths	thousandths

See base, decimal point, place value

decimal point

A point or comma (used in Europe) that separates a decimal fraction from the whole number.

Example: 32 4

↑

decimal point

↓

7 62

See point

decimal system

See decimal place-value system

declination

The slope indicating where an object is compared to a vertical or horizontal position.

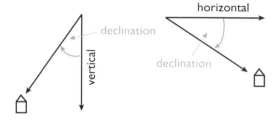

decrease

Make smaller. We either subtract a number or divide by a number.

Examples:
(i)   Decrease this length by 2 cm.

5 cm − 2 cm = 3 cm

We decreased 5 cm to 3 cm by cutting 2 cm off.

(ii) Decrease $100 five times.

$100 ÷ 5 = $20

$100 decreased five times is $20.

See increase, progression

degree

(Symbol: °)

(i) In geometry, a degree is a unit for measuring angles.

Examples:

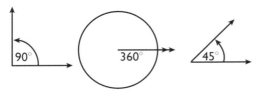

1 degree is divided into 60 minutes
1° (degree) = 60′ (minutes)
1 minute is divided into 60 seconds
1′ (minute) = 60″ (seconds)

(Don't confuse this with the symbols for feet and inches.)

(ii) The unit for measuring temperature.

See angle, degree Celsius, geometry, temperature, unit of measurement

degree Celsius

(Symbol: °C)

The common unit for measuring temperature.

Example:

The boiling point of
water is 100°C.

The old unit was called degree Centigrade.

See temperature, thermometer

denominator

The number written below the line in a vulgar fraction; it tells how many parts there are in the whole.

Example:
This circle has been divided into 6 equal parts.

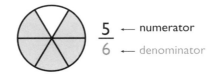

$\frac{5}{6}$ ← numerator
← denominator

In $\frac{5}{6}$ the denominator is 6.
See fraction, numerator

density

(i) The compactness of a material.

(ii) The mass per unit of volume of a material. The relationship of mass to volume. Usually expressed as g/cm³ or kg/m³.

Example:
The density of water at 4°C is 1g/cm³ (one gram per cubic centimetre).

depth

How deep something is. Measurement from the top down, from the front to the back or from the surface inwards.

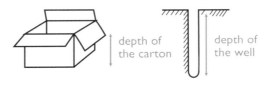

depth of the carton   depth of the well

descending order

Going down or decreasing in value.

Example:
The following lengths have been arranged in descending order:

5.7 m   4.9 m   3.8 m   1.25 m

↑   ↑
longest   shortest

See ascending order, decrease

diagonal

A line segment joining two corners that are not next to each other in any polygon.

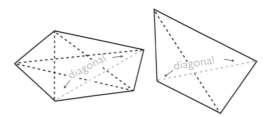

The dotted lines are diagonals.

See polygon

diagram

A name given to pictures or sketches of geometric figures. It is also used for simplified drawings which explain or describe other things.

Examples:

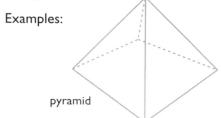

pyramid

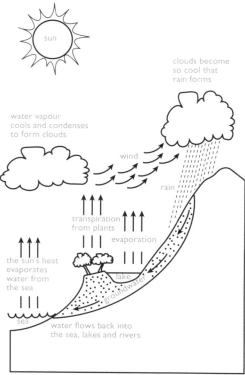

The water cycle

See Carroll diagram

diameter

A line segment joining two points of a circle and passing through the centre of the circle. Diameter equals two radii (r).

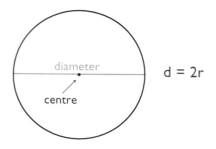

$d = 2r$

See chord, circle, circumference, line segment, radius

diamond

A two-dimensional shape with four equal sides where the angles are not right angles.
The correct name is rhombus.

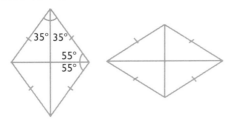

See dimension, rhombus

die

(Plural: dice)

A cube marked with a certain number of spots or numerals. Used in number games.

Examples:

one die   two dice

Some dice have more than 6 faces.

difference

The amount by which two numbers differ.

Example:

$$10 - 3 = 7$$

minuend   subtrahend   difference

The difference between ten and three is seven.

See minuend, subtract, subtraction, subtrahend

digit

Numerals 0, 1, 2, 3, … 9 are called digits; we can also call them one-digit numbers.

Examples:

4 is a one-digit number

56 is a two-digit number

813 is a three-digit number

See place holder, place value

digital clock

A clock or a watch that shows time by numbers. It has no clock hands.

Example:

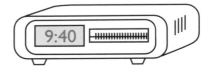

This clock shows twenty to ten.

See a.m., analogue clock, p.m., time interval

dimension

A property that can be measured, related to plane and space.

(i)   One-dimensional (1D) objects have only length.

Examples: lines, curves

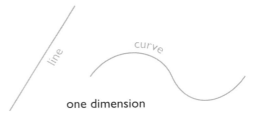

one dimension

(ii) Two-dimensional (2D) objects have length and width.

Examples: plane figures–polygons, circles

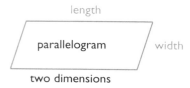

two dimensions

(iii) Three-dimensional (3D) objects have length, width and height.

Examples: solids—cubes, pyramids

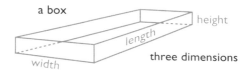

three dimensions

Note: A point (dot) has no dimensions.

See one-dimensional, plane, space, three-dimensional, two-dimensional

direct proportion

See proportion

directed angle

The amount of turning from one ray (or arm of an angle) to the next, used in taking bearings.

Example:

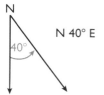

N 40° E

The directed angle (bearing) is N 40° E.

See arm of angle, bearing

directed numbers

Numbers that have + or − signs on them. They are also called integers. We can show them on a number line.

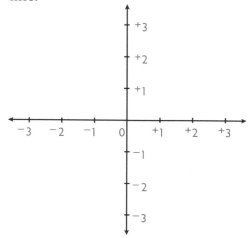

See integers

direction

(i) The way to go.

Examples:

Left, right, up, down, above, below, inside, outside, near, from behind, forwards, backwards, etc.

(ii) Compass directions:

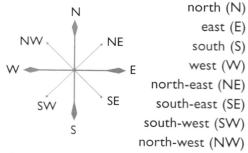

north (N)
east (E)
south (S)
west (W)
north-east (NE)
south-east (SE)
south-west (SW)
north-west (NW)

See anticlockwise, clockwise, compass

displacement

A change in the position of an object or of a quantity of material.

Example:

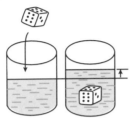

The quantity of water displaced by an immersed object.

The water displacement method is used to measure the volume of objects. The volume of displaced water is equal to the volume of the object.

See volume

distance

The length between one point and another.

Example:

8 cm

Distance between the points of the compasses is 8 centimetres.

3 km

Distance from my house to town is three kilometres.

distribute

Give share of something to each; deal out as in division.

Mum is going to distribute the cakes.

See division

distribution

See frequency distribution

distributive law

$$a\,(b \pm c) = ab \pm ac$$

Every term inside the grouping symbols is multiplied by the term that is immediately outside. This is also called expanding the expression or removing the grouping symbols.

See expand, expanded notation, grouping symbols

dividend

A number which is to be divided by another number.

Example: $24 \div 6 = 4$

dividend divisor quotient

24 is the dividend.

See divisor, quotient

divisibility tests

A number is divisible by another if, after dividing, there is no remainder.

A number is

Divisible by	If	Examples
2	the last digit is even	2, 4, 6, ... 122 ...358 ...1000
3	the sum of all digits can be divided by 3	261 2+6+1=9 3672 3+6+7+2=18 18 1+8=9
4	the last two digits are divisible by 4	1024 24 ÷ 4 = 6
5	the last digit is 5 or 0	15, 70...
7	there is no divisibility test	
8	the last 3 digits are divisible by 8	75 384 384 ÷ 8 = 48
9	the sum of its digits is divisible by 9	3123 3+1+2+3=9
10	the number ends in 0	10, 20, 30...

Important: **No number can be divided by 0.**

See factors, remainder

divisible

A number is divisible by another number if, after dividing, there is no remainder.

Example:
$$72 \div 9 = 8 \qquad 72 \div 8 = 9$$

Seventy-two is divisible by nine and also by eight.

Nine and eight are factors of seventy-two.

See factors, remainder

division

Division is a mathematical operation which can be interpreted in several different ways:

(i)   Grouping (quotition)

Example:

How many groups of 3 can be made with 15 apples?

The apples are to be placed into groups of equal size, 3 to a group. The problem is to find out how many groups there will be.

$$15 \div 3 = 5$$

There are 5 groups of 3 apples.

Repeated subtraction is a form of grouping.

(ii) Sharing (partition)

Example:
Share 15 apples among 5 children. How many apples will each child get?

The apples are to be separated into 5 equal groups. The problem is to find how many there will be in each group.

$$15 \div 5 = 3$$

(iii) Ratio
Comparison between two quantities.

Example:

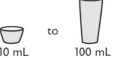 to $10 : 100 = 1 : 10$

10 mL   100 mL

Ratio 1 : 10

Mixing 1 part of cordial and 10 parts of water to make a drink.

See ratio

divisor

A number which is to be divided into another number.

Example:

$$24 \div 6 = 4$$

dividend   divisor   quotient

6 is the divisor.

See dividend, quotient

dodecagon

A polygon with twelve sides.

Examples:

regular dodecagon

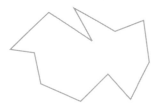

irregular dodecagon

See polygon

dodecahedron

A solid (polyhedron) with twelve faces.
A regular dodecahedron is made by joining together twelve congruent regular pentagons.

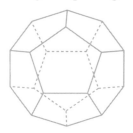

regular dodecahedron

See pentagon, polyhedron, regular polyhedron

dollar

(Symbol: $)

A unit of money.

See cent

dot paper

Paper printed with dots arranged in a pattern. It is used for drawing shapes, defining areas, games, etc., and to record work done on a geo-board.

Examples:

See geo-board, isometric graph paper, square paper

double

Twice as many, or the same again.

Examples:

 is double

Double 8 is 16.

10 is double 5.

dozen

Twelve items.

Example:

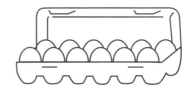

One dozen eggs = twelve eggs

edge

In geometry, the line that is the intersection of two plane faces.

Examples:

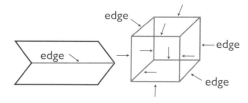

See face, intersection, plane

element of a set

One of the individual objects that belong in (are members of) a set.

Example:

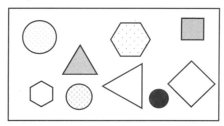

 is an element of the set of shapes.

See cardinal number, set

elevation, angle of

See angle of elevation

ellipse

A closed curve that looks like an elongated circle.

Example:

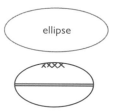

A football is elliptical in shape.

See closed curve

enlargement

Making bigger. Enlargement is the most commonly used transformation. It can be made in many ways: using a grid, rays, by pantograph or a photocopier.

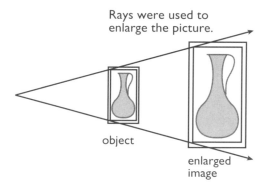

Rays were used to enlarge the picture.

object

enlarged image

See pantograph, reduce, scale drawing, transformation

equal

(Symbol: $=$)

(i) Identical in quantity.

Example:

These two packets of sugar have an equal mass of one kilogram.

(ii) Of the same value.

Example:

$5 note equals five $1 coins.

(iii) The sums $1 + 8 = 3 + 6 =$
$10 - 1 = 2 + 7 =$
$4 + 5 = 9 + 0$
are equal because they are all different ways of writing number 9.

See equality, equal sign

equaliser

A balance with numbered hooks placed at intervals along the beam so that number facts can be represented, and equality indicated, by balance.

Example: A unit mass on the fifth hook on one side would balance unit masses on the second and third hooks on the other side.

$$5 \quad = \quad 2+3$$

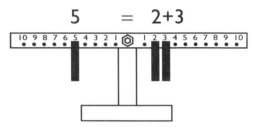

See balance, equality

equality

The relation of being equal.
A statement that two expressions are equal, usually expressed as an equation.

Example:

$$2 + 4 = 6$$

See equal, equation, inequality

equally likely

Events which have the same chance of occurring are said to be equally likely.

Example:

When a die is rolled fairly, the six numbers, 1, 2, 3, 4, 5 and 6, are equally likely to occur.

See chance event, probability

equal sign

(Symbol: =)

The name of the symbol which means 'is equal to' or 'equals'. It shows that:

$$3 + 5 \quad = \quad 8$$

this   is equal to   this

See equal, symbol

---

equation

A statement that two quantities are equal. An equation has two sides which are equal or balanced. There must be the equal sign.

Example:

$x + 4 = 7$

This equation is true only if x has the value of three.

The x and any other signs or letters used in equations to stand for a quantity are called place holders or pronumerals.

See equality, inequation, place holder, pronumeral

---

equilateral

Having sides of equal length.

(i) Square, regular pentagon, hexagon and other regular polygons have sides of equal length and angles of equal size.

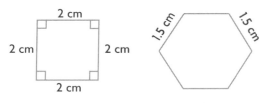

regular hexagon

(ii) equilateral triangle

A triangle which has three sides of equal length and three equal angles.

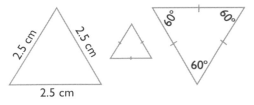

The angles of any equilateral triangle are always 60°.

See triangle

---

equivalent

Having the same value. The same amount.

Example:

A \$2 coin is equivalent to two \$1 coins.

See equivalent fractions

equivalent fractions

Fractions that name the same number or amount.

Example:

Fractions $\frac{1}{2} = \frac{2}{4} = \frac{3}{6} = \frac{4}{8}$ are equivalent

See equivalent, fraction

estimate

(i) A rough or approximate calculation.

(ii) A number that has not been calculated accurately. Estimated answers are often needed when working with decimals.

Example:

In 1.9×3 the estimate will be

$$2 \times 3 = 6$$
$$\therefore 1.9 \times 3 \approx 6$$

(iii) Trying to judge or guess what a measure or result will be.

Example:

The table is 13 handspans long, that is roughly 2 metres.

See accurate, approximate, calculate, rounding

evaluate

To find the value of.

Examples:
(i) Evaluate 21×3

$$\begin{array}{r} 21 \\ \times\ 3 \\ \hline 63 \end{array}$$

The value of 21×3 is 63.

(ii) Evaluate $p + 3q$

Given that $p = 2.5$ and $q = 7$

$$\begin{aligned} p + 3q &= 2.5 + (3 \times 7) \\ &= 2.5 + 21 \\ &= 23.5 \end{aligned}$$

even

Equally balanced, equal in number or amount.

Example:
$5 = \$2.50 + \$1 + \$1.50$

even number

A number that is divisible by two. All even numbers finish with one of the digits: 0, 2, 4, 6 or 8.

See digit, divisible

exact

Precise, accurate, correct in every way, not approximate.

See approximate

exchange

(i) When we go shopping, we exchange money for goods. Money is the medium of exchange.

Example:

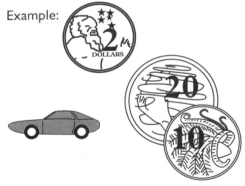

$2.30 is the price of the toy car.

(ii) Multibase Arithmetic Blocks (MAB) can be exchanged.

Example:

units		tens and units
were exchanged for		
16 units	1 ten	6 units

See equivalent, multibase arithmetic blocks, rate

(iii) Money can also be exchanged for money of equivalent value.

Example:

is the same amount as

See equivalent, multibase arithmetic blocks, rate

expand

Write out in full.

Examples:
(i) Expand   4

=

(ii) Expand 537

537 = 500 + 30 + 7

See expanded notation

expanded notation

A way of writing numerals or algebraic expressions.

Examples:

(i) $249 = 200 + 40 + 9$

or $= (2 \times 100) + (4 \times 10) + (9 \times 1)$

or $= 2 \times 10^2 + 4 \times 10^1 + 9 \times 10^0$

(ii) In algebra

$2(a + 2b) = (2 \times a) + (2 \times 2b)$

or $\quad\quad = a + a + b + b + b + b$

See index notation, scientific notation

exponent

A symbol indicating how many times the quantity is to be multiplied by itself to produce the power shown. Another word for index.

See base, index, index notation, power of a number

expression

See algebra

exterior

The outside of something.

Examples:

(i) exterior angle

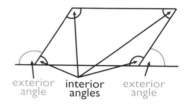

(ii) exterior angle of a triangle

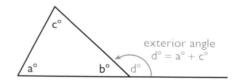

The exterior angle of a triangle is the sum of the two opposite interior angles.

See interior angles

face

In a three-dimensional shape, a face is the flat part of the surface that is bounded by the edges.

Examples:

(i) A cube has six faces.

(ii) A tetrahedron has four faces.

(iii) A pyramid has five faces.

See cube, edge, plane shapes, pyramid, surface, tetrahedron, three-dimensional

factorisation

We can simplify algebraic expressions by extracting a common factor.

Example: Factorise 3a + 6b

$$3a \quad + \quad 6b$$
$$= 3 \times a \quad + \quad 2 \times 3 \times b$$

common factor

$$= \quad 3(a + 2b)$$

See algebraic expression

factors

All the whole numbers that can be divided exactly into another number.

Examples:	factor
(i) $6 \div 1 = 6$	1
$6 \div 2 = 3$	2
$6 \div 3 = 2$	3
$6 \div 6 = 1$	6

1, 2, 3 and 6 are factors of 6.

(ii) $5 \div 1 = 5$
$5 \div 5 = 1$

Prime number 5 has only the factors 5 and 1.

See composite number, factor tree, prime number, whole number

factor tree

A diagram that shows the prime factors of a given number.

Example:

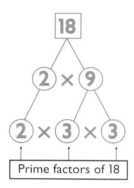

Prime factors of 18

See prime factor of a number

false sentence

A sentence about numbers that is not true.

Examples:
5 < 1 is a false sentence.

The open sentence 3 + ☐ = 10 becomes false, if ☐ is replaced by any other number than 7, e.g. 3, 4, 5 ...

If ☐ is replaced by 7, it will become a true sentence.

See number sentence, true sentence

farthest

(furthest)

The longest distance away.

Example:

Name	Distance
Kate	3.50 m
Paul	3.89 m
Mike	3.47 m

Paul jumped the farthest.

See distance

figure

Another name for a numeral, line, shape or a solid.

Examples:
(i) Write in figures: thirty-six 36

(ii) Half of this figure has been coloured in.

finite

Anything that has boundaries or can be counted.

Examples:
(i) The region inside a square is finite because it is bounded by a perimeter.

(ii) The set of months in a year is a finite set because the months can be counted.

See infinite, perimeter, region, set

first

The one at the beginning, before any other.

Example:

The first shape is a square.

flat

(i) Being in one plane only.

Every face of a
cube is flat

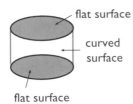

flat surface

curved
surface

flat surface

(ii) The name used for the MAB block representing one hundred.

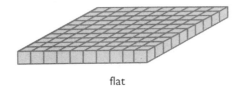

flat

See cube, face, multibase arithmetic blocks (MAB), plane, surface

flexible

A jointed structure is flexible when its angles can be changed by moving the struts without altering their size or arrangement.

Example:

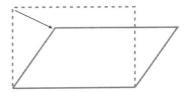

A rectangle forms a flexible structure.

See rigid

flip

To turn over.

Example:

This playing card has
been flipped over.

See reflection, slide, turn

foot

(Plural: feet)
(Symbols: ', ft)

Old imperial measure of length.

1 foot ≈ 30 centimetres
1 foot = 12 inches

formula

(Plural: formulae, formulas)

An equation that uses symbols to represent a statement.

Example:

Statement: The area of a rectangle is found when its length is multiplied by its width.

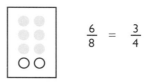

length l

Formula:

$A = l \times w$

See area, equation, symbol

fortnight

Fourteen days or two weeks.

fraction

A part of a whole quantity or number.

Examples:

(i) The fraction $\frac{3}{4}$ means 3 parts out of a total of 4 equal parts.

$\frac{3}{4}$

3 parts out of 4 parts are coloured

(ii) 7 parts out of 100 parts are coloured in.

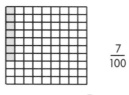

$\frac{7}{100}$

The fraction is $\frac{7}{100}$.

(iii) Show $\frac{3}{4}$ of 8.

$\frac{6}{8} = \frac{3}{4}$

See cancelling, common denominator, decimal fraction, equivalent fraction, improper fraction, mixed number, proper fraction, simple fraction

frequency

The frequency of any item in a collection of data is the number of times that item occurs in the collection.

Example:

We tossed a die 50 times and recorded the number for each throw. We kept a tally of the 50 scores.

Number	Tally	Frequency
1	II	7
2	II	12
3	IIII	9
4	III	8
5	I	6
6	III	8

Number 2 had the highest frequency

Number 5 had the lowest frequency

See data, frequency distribution, tally

frequency distribution

A graph or table showing how often an event or quantity occurs.

Example:

A Frequency Distribution Table of Marks:

Mark	Tally	Frequency
20–29	I	1
30–39	₩	5
40–49	₩ IIII	9
50–59	₩ III	8
60–69	₩	5
70–79	III	3
80–89	I	1
	Total	32

frequency table

See frequency distribution

front view

A diagram of an object, as seen from directly in front of it.

Example:

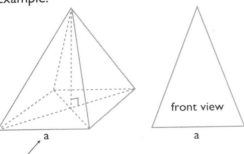

front view

See cross-section, plan, side view

frustum

A pyramid cut by a plane parallel to the pyramid's base.

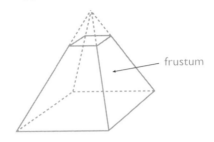

frustum

See decahedron, pyramid, section

g

(i)　g is the symbol for the unit gram.

(ii)　It is also a symbol for gravity. The force of gravity on the earth's surface is 1 g.

See mass, newton, weight

geo-board

A board studded with nails forming a pattern or grid, usually of squares or equilateral triangles. Geo-boards are used for shape and number activities in which elastic bands are arranged around sets of nails.

See equilateral triangle, grid, pattern

geometric progression

See progression

geometry

The part of mathematics that deals with the relationships, properties and measurements of solids, surfaces, lines, angles and space.

See measure, property, solid, space, surface

geo-strips

Strips of plastic, metal or cardboard with holes equally spaced down the centre of the strips. They are used for making shapes.

Examples:

one geo-strip

Shapes made using geo-strips.

See flexible, rigid

Goldbach's conjecture

Every even, natural number is equal to the sum of two prime numbers.

$2 = 1 + 1$	$10 = 3 + 7$
$4 = 2 + 2$	$12 = 5 + 7$ or $1 + 11$
$6 = 3 + 3$	$24 = 11 + 13$
$8 = 1 + 7$	$42 = 19 + 23$

See natural numbers, prime numbers

googol

A very large number. It has the numeral 1 with one hundred zeros after it.

1 000 000 000 000 000 000 000
     000 000 000 000 000 000 000
     000 000 000 000 0 ...

gradient

Measurement of slope, inclination to horizontal, or the pitch. It is measured and expressed as a ratio.

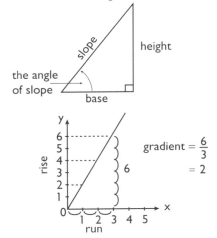

The ratio $\frac{\text{height}}{\text{base}}$ or $\frac{\text{rise}}{\text{run}}$ is called the slope, the gradient or the pitch.

graduated

Marked off with measurements.

Examples:

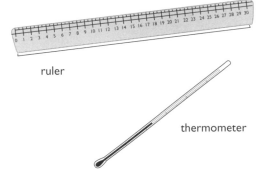

ruler

thermometer

A thermometer is graduated in degrees.

A ruler is graduated in centimetres.

gram
(Symbol: g)

A unit of mass.
1000 g = 1 kg

Examples:

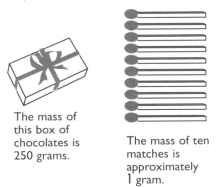

The mass of this box of chocolates is 250 grams.

The mass of ten matches is approximately 1 gram.

See mass, unit of measurement

graph 58

graph

Drawings or diagrams which show information, usually about how many things.
There are different kinds of graphs.

Examples:

BIRTHDAY GRAPH

JAN	Jessica, Nao
FEB	Kate, Ben, Ian
MAR	Tom, Hirani
APR	Sue, Mary, Paul
MAY	Tim, Joe, Xavier
JUN	Jim, Paula, Mia, Sam
JUL	Lena, Lucy, Tibor
AUG	Sonia, Ted, James
SEPT	Chris, Quong
OCT	Kim, Ann, Kelly
NOV	Ken, Halima
DEC	Paul, Helen, Judy, Carl

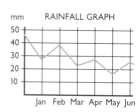

This is a line graph

See axis, bar graph, column graph, line graph, pictograph, pie graph

greater than

(Symbol: >)

A relation between a pair of numbers showing which is greater. More than. Bigger than.

Example:

7 > 6

greater than

See less than

grid

Regular lines that go across, up and down. Often found on maps and graphs.

Examples:

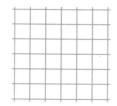

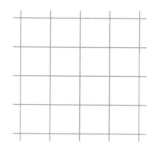

See isometric paper, square paper

gross

Twelve dozen, 144.

gross mass

The mass of an object together with its container.

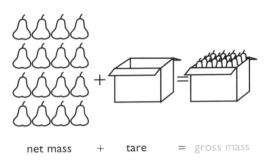

net mass   +   tare   = gross mass

The actual mass of the object is called net mass. The mass of the container is called tare.

See mass

group

(i)   Putting things together in a set or group. In the decimal system things are grouped into tens.

Hundreds	Tens	Units
2	4	3

243 = 2 groups of 100
        4 groups of 10
        3 groups of 1

(ii) Two or more things.

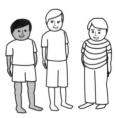

A group of boys.

See grouping

grouping

Putting things together into sets with the same number in each set.

Example:

How many groups of four can be made with twenty balls?

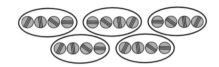

Answer: Twenty balls are put into five groups of four.

See division, set

grouping symbols

See brackets

h

Symbol for height, hour, prefix hecto-.

ha

A symbol for hectare.

half

(Plural: halves)

One part of two equal parts.

Examples:

(i) half $= \dfrac{1}{2}$

(ii) Half of twenty-four is twelve.

$$\dfrac{1}{2} \times 24 = 12$$

(iii) An orange has been cut into two halves

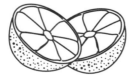

handspan

The distance from the top of the thumb to the top of the smallest finger when the hand is fully stretched.

Example:

This is a handspan.

A handspan is used as an arbitrary measure for estimating the lengths, heights or widths of objects.

See arbitrary unit, estimate

hectare

(Symbol: ha)

A unit of area.
One hectare is the area of a square with sides measuring 100 metres.

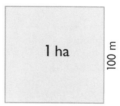

The area of a soccer field is approximately half a hectare.

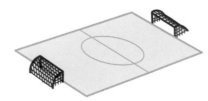

See area, unit of measurement

heft

To judge the weight of objects by lifting them in the hands.

Examples:

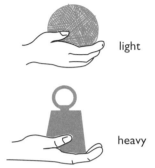

light

heavy

See weight

height

Measurement from top to bottom, the vertical distance.

Examples:

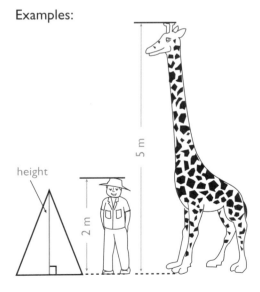

See altitude, vertical

hemisphere

Half of a sphere.

Example: Australia lies in the southern hemisphere.

Each part is $\frac{1}{2}$ of a sphere

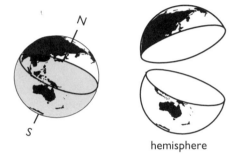

hemisphere

See sphere

heptagon

A polygon with seven sides and seven angles. Regular heptagons have all sides congruent and all angles the same.

regular heptagon

irregular heptagon

See polygon

hexagon

A shape (polygon) which has six sides and six angles.

Examples:

regular hexagon

irregular hexagons

Honeycomb is made up of regular hexagons.

See polygon

hexagram

A shape formed by two intersecting equilateral triangles.

hexahedron

A solid (polyhedron) with six faces. All cuboids are hexahedrons. A cube is a regular hexahedron; all six faces are congruent squares, all internal angles are equal.

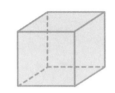

regular hexahedron

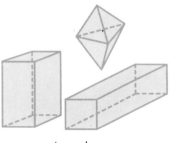

irregular hexahedrons

See cube, cuboid, polyhedron, prism, regular polyhedron

highest common factor
(HCF)

The largest number that divides into all given numbers.

Example:

For given numbers 8, 12, 16 and 20 the highest common factor (HCF) is 4.

See factors, factor tree

Hindu–Arabic

Our modern system of numbers is the result of centuries of development.

The symbols for all the digits, except zero, probably originated with the Hindus in India, as early as 200 BC.

Hindu numerals

٢ ٢ ٣ ৪ ५ ६ ७ ८ ६

The Arabs adopted the system. Arabic numerals (13th century AD.)

⁰ ١ 2 3 4 ১ 6 7 ৪ 9

The numerals, including zero, were standardised after the invention of the printing press in the 15th century.

0 1 2 3 4 5 6 7 8 9

The modern system has very useful characteristics:
1　It has only ten digits: 0, 1, 2, 3, 4, ...9.
2　It uses zero to mark an empty space.
3　It uses place value system; the value of the number depends on placement in the numeral:
　　37　　307　　13 700

See numeral, place value

histogram

A column graph with no spaces between columns.

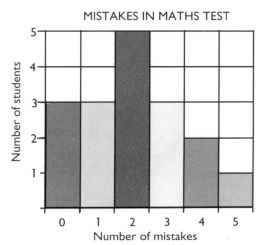

MISTAKES IN MATHS TEST

See column, column graph

horizon

Line at which land and sky appear to meet.

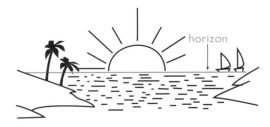

See horizontal line

horizontal line

Line parallel to, or on a level with, the horizon.

A vertical line is at right angles to the horizon.

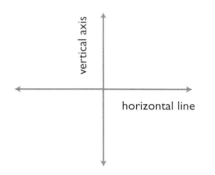

See axis, bar graph, base line, parallel, right angle, vertical

horizontal surface

Any surface which is parallel to, or on a level with, the horizon.

Examples:

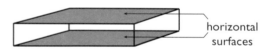

See horizon, parallel, surface

hour

(Symbol: h)

A unit of time.

1 hour = 60 minutes

1 hour = 3600 seconds

24 hours = 1 day

See unit of measurement

hypotenuse

The longest side of a right-angled triangle, which is the side directly opposite the right angle.

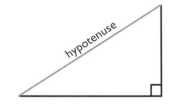

See Pythagoras' theorem, right-angled triangle

image

An exact copy of an object.

Example:

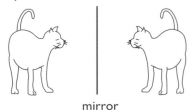

mirror

The image in a mirror.

See mapping, mirror image, reflection

icosahedron

A solid (polyhedron) with twenty faces.
A regular icosahedron is formed by joining together twenty congruent equilateral triangles.

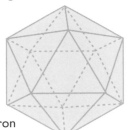

regular icosahedron

See polyhedron, regular polyhedron

improper fraction

A fraction whose numerator is greater than its denominator.

Example:

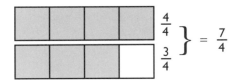

$\left. \begin{array}{c} \frac{4}{4} \\ \frac{3}{4} \end{array} \right\} = \frac{7}{4}$

See denominator, fraction, mixed number, numerator, proper fraction

identical

Exactly alike.

Examples:

5   5

inch
(Symbol: ″)

Old imperial measure of length.

1 inch ≈ 2.5 cm

12 inches = 1 foot

increase

Make larger by adding a certain amount, or multiplying by a number.

Examples:

(i) The price of a one dollar bus ticket has been increased by twenty cents.

$1 + 20c = $1.20

(ii) My family of 2 cats has increased 3 times. How many kittens do I have now?

2 x 3 = 6

6 − 2 = 4
I have 4 kittens.

See decrease, progression

index

(Plural: indices)

$$5^3$$
index or exponent

base

Index is also called exponent.

In $^3\sqrt{5}$ the index is 3. Where no index is written, as in $\sqrt{5}$, the index is 2.

See base, exponent, index notation, square root

index laws

In algebra, when working with indices or algebraic expressions, these laws must be remembered:

Law:	Example:
$x^a \times x^b = x^{a+b}$	$5^3 \times 5^2 = 5^{3+2} = 5^5$
$\dfrac{x^a}{x^b} = x^{a-b}$	$\dfrac{5^3}{5^2} = 5^{3-2} = 5^1 = 5$
$x^0 = 1$	$5^0 = 1$
$(x^a)^b = x^{a \times b} = x^{ab}$	$(5^3)^2 = 5^{3 \times 2} = 5^6$
$(x \times y)^a = x^a y^a$	$(5 \times 4)^3 = 5^3 \times 4^3$
$\left(\dfrac{x}{y}\right)^a = \dfrac{x^a}{y^a}$	$\left(\dfrac{5}{4}\right)^3 = \dfrac{5^3}{4^3}$
$x^{-a} = \dfrac{1}{x^a}$	$5^{-3} = \dfrac{1}{5^3}$
$^n\sqrt{a} = a^{\frac{1}{n}}$	$^3\sqrt{5} = 5^{\frac{1}{3}}$

index notation

A shorthand way of writing large numbers such as 1 000 000. Also called scientific notation.
Using index notation:
1 000 000 = 10 × 10 × 10 × 10 × 10 × 10 = 10^6

$$10^6$$
index or exponent

base

is read as:
'ten to the power of six' or 'ten to the sixth power'.

See base, cubed number, power of a number, scientific notation, squared number

inequality

A statement that one quantity is less than or greater than another. The symbols $<$, $>$ and $\neq$ are used to express inequalities.

Examples:
$5 \neq 6$　Five is not equal to six.
$5 < 6$　Five is less than 6.
$6 > 4$　Six is greater than 4.

See equality, greater than, less than, not equal

inequality signs

Sign:	Meaning:
$<$	less than
$\leq$	less than or equal to
$\neq$	not equal to
$>$	greater than
$\geq$	greater than or equal to

inequation

A statement that two quantities are not equal.

Example:

$$x + 5 > 7$$
$${-5}\quad{-5}$$
$$\underline{x > 2}$$

This inequation is true for any number greater than 2, for example 3, because $3 + 5 = 8$, which is greater than 7.

See equality, equation, inequality

infer

Make a predictive statement or conclusion, based on observation or reasoning.

See prediction

infinite

Without bounds of size or number, unlimited, not finite, endless.

Example:
{Whole numbers} is an infinite set.

See finite, set, whole number

infinite decimal

(not terminating)

Decimals which go on without an end.

Example:
$\pi = 3.141\ 592\ 7...$

See recurring decimal, terminating decimal

infinity

(Symbol: ∞)

Expressing quantity without bounds.

See infinite

input

See number machine

insignificant zeros

Unnecessary zeros in decimal numbers.

Example:

wrong	correct
$\underline{0}5.2$	5.2
$9.98\underline{0}$	9.98
.25	0.25

integers

Positive or negative whole numbers including zero.

Examples:

Integers

negative   positive

The set of integers:

$\{\ldots-6, -5, -4, -3, -2, -1, 0, 1, 2, 3, 4, 5\ldots\}$

See directed, negative and positive numbers, set, whole number

intercept

When drawing graphs of equations, an intercept is the point where the equation line crosses an axis.

Example:

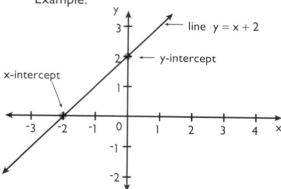

The line $y = x + 2$ crosses the y-axis at point $(0, 2)$. The point $(0, 2)$ is called the y-intercept.

The line also crosses the x-axis at point $(-2, 0)$, which is called the x-intercept.

See coordinates, gradient

interior

The inside of something.

See exterior

interior angles

Angles inside a shape.

Example:

The sum of interior angles inside any triangle is 180°.

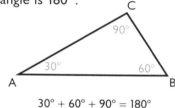

$30° + 60° + 90° = 180°$

intersect

To cut across. To cross each other.

Example:

The two lines intersect at point A.

intersection

(i) The place where two or more lines meet, like an intersection of two streets.

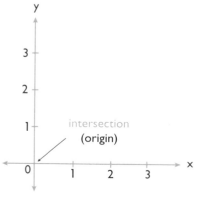

(ii) The region where shapes overlap.

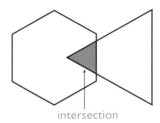

intersection

(iii) (Of sets) The set of elements that are common to both sets.

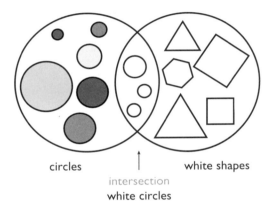

circles   white shapes
intersection
white circles

See coordinates, origin, region, set, shape

interval

The amount of time, or distance, between two events or places.

Examples:

(i) There is a twenty minute interval between the two films.

(ii) Line segment.

line
interval

See line

inverse

Inverted in position, order or relation. When one quantity increases, the other decreases at the same rate.

See additive inverse, proportion, ratio

inverse factor tree

A diagram that shows prime numbers and the number they belong to.

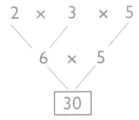

Prime numbers: 2, 3 and 5 have a product of 30.

See factor tree, prime factor of a number

inverse operations

The operation which reverses the action of the original operation.

Examples:
The operations
4 + 3 = 7 and
7 − 3 = 4
are the inverse of one another.

The operations
6 × 3 = 18 and
18 ÷ 3 = 6
are the inverse of one another.

See operation, reciprocal

invert

Turn upside down, reverse position.

$\frac{1}{2}$ inverts to $\frac{2}{1}$ or 2

$\frac{3}{4}$ inverts to $\frac{4}{3}$ or $1\frac{1}{3}$

irrational numbers

Numbers that cannot be written as integers or ratios.
Examples:

$$\pi, \quad \sqrt{2}, \quad \sqrt{3}, \quad \sqrt[3]{2}$$

See rational numbers, real numbers

irregular polygon

A shape in which not all sides are equal in length, and/or at least one angle is different in size from the other angles.

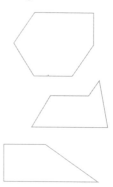

See polygon, regular polygon

isometric drawing

A drawing where the three dimensions are represented by three sets of lines 120° apart, and all measurements are in the same scale (not in perspective).

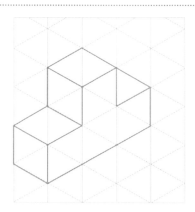

See perspective

isometric graph paper

Paper with dots or lines that make equilateral triangles. Used for isometric drawings.

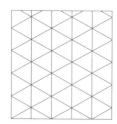

See equilateral triangle, square paper

isosceles triangle

A triangle in which two sides have the same length and two angles have the same size.

Examples:

2.5 cm, 2.5 cm, 2.5 cm

3 cm, 3 cm, 65°, 65°, 2.5 cm

jigsaw

A puzzle in which pieces fit together to form a picture.

joule

Unit of energy or work. It replaces the old unit, calorie.

See kilojoule

kilogram

(Symbol: kg)

The base unit of mass.

1 kg = 1000 g

Examples:
The mass of this packet of sugar is one kilogram.

The mass of this girl is twenty-seven kilograms.

See gram, mass, unit of measurement

kilojoule

(Symbol: kJ)

Used for measuring energy or work.

1 kilojoule = 1000 joules

Example:

A piece of chocolate cake has 2000 kilojoules.

kilolitre

(Symbol: kL)

A unit of volume (capacity) for measuring liquids.

$$1 \text{ kL} = 1000 \text{ L}$$

Example:

Five 200 litre oil drums hold one kilolitre.

See capacity, unit of measurement, volume

kilometre

(Symbol: km)

A unit of distance. Distances between towns are measured in kilometres.

$$1 \text{ km} = 1000 \text{ m}$$

Example:

The road distance from Darwin to Katherine is 352 kilometres.

See distance, unit of measurement

kite

A quadrilateral is shaped like this.

The two short sides are equal in length. The two long sides are equal in length. The diagonals are perpendicular to each other.

See quadrilateral

knot

(Symbol: kn)

The measure of speed at sea, equal to travelling one nautical mile per hour.

1 nautical mile = 1.852 kilometres

Example:

A ship moving at twenty knots is travelling as fast as a vehicle on land travelling about thirty-seven kilometres per hour.

L

(i)   L is the symbol for litre.
(ii) In Roman numerals L stands for fifty.

See capacity, litre

lateral

See equilateral

LCD

See lowest common denominator

LCM

See lowest common multiple

leap year

A year which has 366 days instead of 365 days. It occurs every four years.
In a leap year February has twenty-nine days instead of twenty-eight days.
When the year number can be divided by 4 leaving no remainder, then it is a leap year.

Examples:
1979 ÷ 4 = 494 (r 3)
This is not a leap year.
1980 ÷ 4 = 495
This is a leap year.

Century years are not leap years unless they are divisible by 400.

Example:
1600, 2000, 2400 are leap years.
1500, 1700, 1800 are not leap years.

least

The smallest thing or amount in a group.

Example:

The toy car costs the least amount.

length

How long something is from end to end.
(i)   The measure of distance.

Examples:

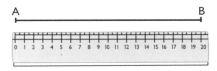

This ruler is twenty centimetres long.

The length of this table is 1.8 metres.

Units of length are:

millimetre	mm
centimetre	cm
metre	m
kilometre	km

(ii) An interval of time.

Example:

How long is the lunchtime break?

See centimetre, distance, interval, kilometre, metre, millimetre

less than

(Symbol: $<$)

A relation between pairs of numbers showing which is smaller.

Example:

$$5 < 7$$
↑
less than

See greater than, inequality signs

like terms

Similar, resembling each other. In algebra, expressions are called like terms if they have the same variable and power. Like terms can be added and subtracted; terms that are not like cannot.

Examples:

Like terms	Unlike terms

$4x - 3x$	$a - b$
$5x^2y + x^2y$	$3x^2 + 3$

See power, unlike terms, variable

line

A long thin mark drawn on a surface. It can be straight or curved. It has no thickness and has only one dimension. A straight line extends without end in both directions.

 a

A straight line is the shortest possible distance between two points.

Example:

A　　　　　B

The line between A and B is the shortest distance between A and B. The arrowheads indicate that the line does not end where we stop drawing it. The interval AB has a finite length.

See curve, horizontal line, infinite, interval, line segment, vertical

linear

Involving measurement in one dimension only.

See line

linear equation

An equation that can be presented as a straight line.

Examples:

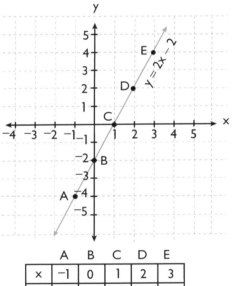

	A	B	C	D	E
x	−1	0	1	2	3
y	−4	−2	0	2	4

$y = 2x − 2$

See equation

line graph

A graph formed by segments of straight lines that join the points representing certain data.

Example:

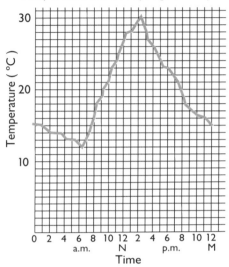

Temperature at Alice Springs on 1 April

See graph, line, line segment

line of symmetry

The line which divides something in half so that one half is the mirror image of the other half. This line is sometimes called an axis of symmetry.
A shape may have more than one line of symmetry.

Examples:

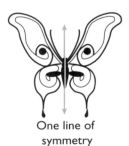

One line of symmetry

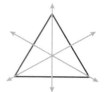

Three lines of
symmetry

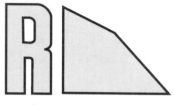

Some shapes have no
line symmetry

See asymmetry, axis, symmetry

line segment

Part of a straight line.

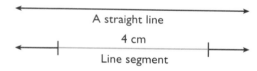

A straight line

4 cm

Line segment

See diameter, line

litre

(Symbol: L)

A unit of capacity used to measure
the volume of liquids or the
capacity of containers.

$$1 \text{ L} = 1000 \text{ cm}^3 = 1000 \text{ mL}$$

$$1000 \text{ L} = 1 \text{ kL}$$

Example:

A carton of milk holds one litre.

See capacity, unit of measurement, volume

lowest common denominator
(LCD)

The lowest counting number that
is divisible by the denominators of
given fractions. The lowest
multiple of two or more
denominators.

Example:
What is the LCD of fractions $\frac{1}{4}$
and $\frac{1}{10}$?

4 divides exactly into   } 4, 8, 12, 16, (20), 24,
(Multiples of 4 are)   } 28, 32, (36), 40, 44....

10 divides exactly into } 10, (20), 30, (40), 50,
(Multiples of 10 are)   }   60, 70....

The lowest number into which 4 and
10 divide exactly is 20.

Therefore 20 is the LCD.
Lowest common denominators are
used in addition and subtraction of
fractions.

Example:

$$\frac{1}{4} + \frac{1}{10} = \frac{5+2}{20} = \frac{7}{20}$$

See common denominator, counting number, denominator, fraction, lowest common multiple

....

lowest common multiple

(LCM)

The lowest counting number that is a multiple of given numbers.

Example:

What is the LCM of 2 and 3?

The multiples of 2 are:

2, 4, ⑥, 8, 10, ⑫, 14, 16, ⑱ ...

The multiples of 3 are:

3, ⑥, 9, ⑫, 15, ⑱, 21, 24 ...

Common multiples are: 6, 12, 18 ...

The lowest common multiple of 2 and 3 is 6.

See counting number, multiple

magnitude

The size, or how big something is.

Example:

The magnitude of this angle is 60°.

See directed numbers

m

(i) m is the symbol for metre.
(ii) m is also the symbol for prefix milli-.

M

(i) M is the symbol for prefix mega-.
(ii) In Roman numerals M means 1000.

MAB

See multibase arithmetic blocks

magic square

A puzzle where the numbers are arranged in a square so that each row, column and diagonal add up to the same total.

Example:

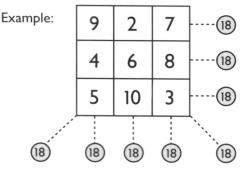

many-to-one correspondence

A match between members of two sets in which more than one element of the first set is associated with one element of the second. Arrows are used to show the relationship.

Example:

Children and their favourite drinks

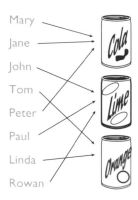

Three elements (Mary, Jane and Peter) of the first set are associated with one element (Cola) of the second set.

See arrow diagram, one-to-one correspondence

mapping

A matching operation between two sets in which each member of the first set is assigned only one member of the second set as a partner or image.

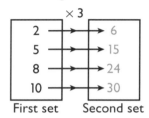

First set   Second set

In the above example, 2 maps onto 6, so 6 is the image of 2.

See image, many-to-one correspondence, one-to-one correspondence, set

mass

The amount of matter contained in an object.

Units of mass:

gram   g

kilogram   kg

tonne   t

1000 g = 1 kg

1000 kg = 1 t

Example:
This boy has a mass of twenty-eight kilograms.

The word 'weight' is commonly but incorrectly used instead of mass.

See beam balance, unit of measurement, weight

matching

See many-to-one correspondence, one-to-one correspondence

mathematical shorthand

Instead of long sentences, mathematics uses numbers, symbols, formulas and diagrams.

Example:
The sentence,
'The area of a triangle is found when its base is multiplied by its perpendicular height and then divided by two,'
is written in mathematical shorthand as:

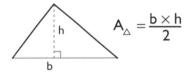

See formula

maximum

The greatest or biggest value.

Examples:
1   The maximum temperature this month was 39° Celsius.

2   The maximum speed is 110 kilometres per hour.

See minimum

maze

A kind of puzzle in which a person has to find a way through a network of lines, paths, etc.

Example:

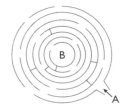

Follow the path from A to B without crossing any lines.

mean

The mean is the average of a set of scores. It is found by adding up all scores and dividing the sum by the number of scores.

Mean = $\frac{\text{sum of scores}}{\text{number of scores}}$

See average, measures of central tendency

measure

(i) Find out the size of something.

Examples:

How long? How tall? How heavy? How hot?

(ii) Compare quantities. A number assigned to a quantity which indicates its size compared to a chosen unit.

Example:

The length of the book is thirty centimetres.

See unit of measurement

measures of central tendency

The three measures are: mode, median and mean. They usually lie about the middle of the distribution and tell us certain facts about it.

See mean, median, mode

median

In statistics, median is the middle measurement or score, when items are arranged in order of size.

Example:

Scores 2, 2, 4, 5, 6, 8, 10

median = 5

Where there is no middle score, an average of the two central scores is taken.

Example:

Scores 2, 3, 4, 8, 9, 10

median = $\frac{4 + 8}{2}$ = 6

See average, mean, measurements of central tendency, mode, score

megalitre

(Symbol: ML)

A unit of capacity.

1 megalitre = 1 000 000 litres

1 ML = 1 000 000 L

Example:
Volume (capacity) of this swimming pool is:

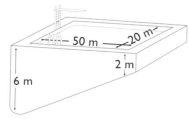

Volume = [50 × 20 × (6 − 2)] m³

= 4000 m³

= 4 000 000 L

= 4 ML

This swimming pool contains four megalitres (4 ML) of water.

mensuration

The branch of mathematics concerned with the measurement of lengths, areas and volumes.

metre

(Symbol: m)

The base unit of length (distance).

1 m = 100 cm

1 m = 1000 mm

Example

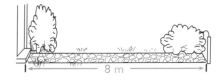

The path is eight metres long.

See distance, unit

metric system

A decimal system of weights and measures. The base unit for length is metre, for mass is kilogram, and for time is second in the international metric system (SI).

See decimal system, SI, unit, basic, unit of measurement

midpoint

A point in the middle of an interval.

Example: $\overline{AM} = \overline{MB}$

The point M is the midpoint of the interval AB.

See bisect, bisector

mile

An old imperial measure of length.
1 mile ≈ 1.6 km

mileage

The distance travelled during which the car uses a certain amount of petrol. It used to mean miles per gallon of petrol. It now means the number of kilometres per litre of petrol, or consumption of petrol per 100 kilometres.

milligram

(Symbol: mg)

A very small unit of mass, used when working with medicines and chemicals. It is one-thousandth of a gram.

$$1 \text{ mg} = \tfrac{1}{1000} \text{ g}$$
$$1 \text{ mg} = 0.001 \text{ g}$$

See gram

millilitre

(Symbol: mL)

A unit of capacity.

1000 mL = 1 L

Note: One millilitre of water at four degrees Celsius has a mass of one gram.

a teaspoon holds 5 mL

a bucket holds 12 L

See centimetre, volume

millimetre

(Symbol: mm)

A unit of length.

10 mm = 1 cm

1 mm

| | | | | | | | | | | | | | | | | | | | | |
0   10 mm   40   50

See centimetre, length

million

One thousand thousands: 1 000 000.

See billion

minimum

The smallest or least value.

Example:

The minimum temperature in July was 4° Celsius.

See maximum

minuend

A number from which another number is to be subtracted.

Example:

$$29 - 7 = 22$$

minuend   subtrahend   difference

29 is the minuend.

See difference, subtract, subtrahend

minus

(Symbol: −)

(i) Subtract or take away.

Example:

Eight minus two is written as 8 − 2 and means two subtracted from eight.

8 − 2 = 6

(ii) A symbol to mark negative numbers.

Example: ⁻1, ⁻2, ⁻3, ⁻4…

See integers, negative numbers, subtract

minute

(Symbol: min)

(i) A measure of time.
     One minute = sixty seconds
     1 min   = 60 s

There are sixty minutes in one hour.

(ii) Angle measurement

$1 \text{ min} = \frac{1}{60}^{\circ}$ (degree)

1° (degree) = 60 min

mirror image

A reflection, as in a mirror.

See image, reflection

mixed number

A whole number and a fraction.

Examples:

$1\frac{1}{2}$ $3\frac{5}{2}$

This is another way of writing an improper fraction:

$\frac{3}{2} = 1\frac{1}{2}$ $\frac{35}{30} = 1\frac{5}{30} = 1\frac{1}{6}$

See fraction, improper fraction, whole number

möbius strip

(moebius)

A surface with only one side. It is made by giving a strip of paper or any other flexible material a half twist and then fastening the ends together.

If a line is drawn down the middle of the strip, it will come back to the starting point, having covered both sides of the strip, without the pencil being lifted.

Example:

A thin strip of paper...   can be given a twist...

and have the ends...   joined to make a moebius strip.

mode

In statistics, the score that occurs most often in a collection.

Example:

In scores,
1, 1, 2, 4, 4, 6, 6, 6, 6, 7, 7, 7, 8, 10,

6 is the mode

See average, mean, measures of central tendency, median

model

A three-dimensional representation of an actual or designed object. It may be a physical structure, for example, a model of a cube made from cardboard.

Examples:

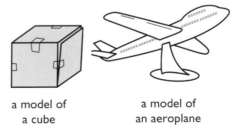

a model of   a model of
a cube   an aeroplane

See cube, net, three-dimensional, scale drawing

month

A measure of time. There are twelve months in a year. The lengths of different months vary from twenty-eight to thirty-one days.

An easy way to remember the number of days in each month is to learn the following rhyme.

> Thirty days has September,
>
> April, June and November.
>
> All the rest have thirty-one,
>
> Except for February alone,
>
> Which has but twenty-eight days clear,
>
> And twenty-nine in each leap year.

See calendar, day, leap year, year

more

Greater in amount.

Example:
Four dollars is more than three dollars.

most

The greatest amount.

Example:

Jim has twenty cents.
Betty has thirty-five cents.
Peter has thirty cents.
Betty has the most.

multibase arithmetic blocks (MAB)

A set of wooden blocks used to give a concrete representation of numbers. They can be used for any base.

Example:
Base 3 blocks

unit   long   flat   cube

The most commonly used MAB blocks are the base ten blocks. A set of base ten blocks consists of:

 small cubes – units or ones

longs – 10 small cubes joined together

flats or squares – 100 small cubes formed into a square

 large cubes – 1000 small cubes formed into a large cube

See base

multilateral

Having many sides.

multiple

A multiple of a given number is any number into which it will divide exactly.

Examples:

Multiples of two are 2, 4, 6, 8, 10, 12 …

Multiples of three are 3, 6, 9, 12, 15, 18 …

Multiples of four are 4, 8, 12, 16, 20, 24 …

See division, lowest common multiple

multiplicand

The number that is to be multiplied.

Example:

$$8 \times 7 = 56$$

multiplicand　multiplier　product

See multiplication, multiplier, product

multiplication

(Symbol: ×)

Multiplication is repeated addition.

 means:

(i)　2 groups of 3,
　　　$2 \times 3 = 6$ or
(ii)　3 multiplied by 2,
　　　$3 \times 2 = 6$ or
(iii) 3 made 2 times bigger.

Sign × refers to two operations:
(i)　lots of or groups of, and
(ii)　multiplied by.

See addition, operation

multiplication facts

See table

multiplication property of one

When a number is multiplied by one, the product is equal to the original number. This is the multiplication property of one.

Examples:

$7 \times 1 = 7$

$1 \times 138 = 138$

Use of the property is made when a fraction is converted to an equivalent form.

Example:

$$\frac{2}{3} = \frac{\square}{12}$$

$$\frac{2}{3} \times 1 = \frac{2}{3} \times \frac{4}{4}$$

$$= \frac{8}{12}$$

$\frac{2}{3}$ has been multiplied by one

(or by $\frac{4}{4}$ which is equal to one)

See equivalent fraction

multiplier

The number by which another number is multiplied.

Example:

$$5 \times 7 = 35$$

multiplicand　multiplier　product

See multiplicand, multiplication, product

multiply

Carry out the process of repeated addition or multiplication.

See addition, multiplication

natural number

One of the counting numbers.

Examples:

1, 2, 3, 4, 5, 6, 7, 8, 9 ...

See counting number, positive numbers

nautical mile

Used to measure travel at sea. One nautical mile equals 1852 metres or 1.852 kilometres.

See knot

negative number

A negative number is a number less than zero. Negative numbers are written with the minus sign (⁻) in front of them.

Examples:

⁻0.1, ⁻0.2, ... ⁻0.9, ... ⁻1, ⁻1.1, ...
⁻2, ... ⁻2.55 ...

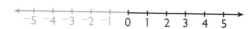

See integers, minus, positive numbers, zero

net

A flat pattern which can be cut out, folded and glued together to make a three-dimensional model of a solid.

Examples:

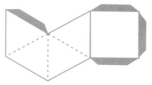

a net of a cube

cube

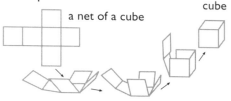

net of a pyramid

pyramid

See cube, model, pattern, pyramid, table of nets

net mass

The mass of an object without packaging.

See gross mass

network

A system of lines or arcs and intersections (nodes) drawn to represent paths and their intersections.

Examples:

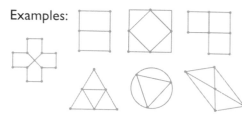

The properties of networks are studied as part of topology.

See intersection, node, topology

node

A point where straight lines or curves intersect. It is also called a junction.

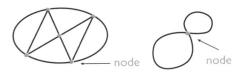

See intersect, network

nonagon

A polygon with nine sides and nine angles.

Examples:

regular nonagon

irregular nonagons

See polygon

none

Nothing. Not one. Not any.

Example:

I have two apples

I have none

See zero

non-planar figure

A three-dimensional figure. A solid or space figure.

Examples:

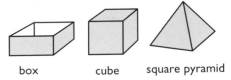

box   cube   square pyramid

Non-planar means 'not in one plane'.

See planar figure

not equal

(Symbol: ≠)

$$4 \neq 5$$

Four is not equal to five.

See inequality

nothing

(Symbol: 0)

Not one. Having not a thing. Not anything. None.

number

How many things. A measure of quantity.
Numbers are grouped into many different sets:

(i) Natural (counting) numbers:
     1, 2, 3, 4, 5, 6, ...

(ii) Whole numbers:
     0, 1, 2, 3, 4, 5, ...

(iii) Integers:
     ... ⁻4, ⁻3, ⁻2, ⁻1, 0, ⁺1, ⁺2, ⁺3, ...

(iv) Rational numbers, which
include fractions:

$1 : 3$ $\frac{1}{100}$

Other kinds of numbers include
complex, composite, prime, odd,
even, square, triangular,
rectangular numbers, etc.

See composite number, even number,
irrational numbers, integer, natural
number, odd number, prime number,
rational number, rectangular number,
square number, triangular number, whole
number

number expander

A folded strip of paper used to
learn place value.

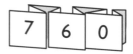

number line

A line on which equally spaced
points are marked. The points
correspond, in order, to the
numbers shown.

Example:

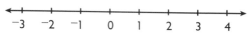

On a number line, the points are
labelled from zero. The numbers
show the distance from zero to
each point (using the distance
between successive points as one
unit).

Operations with numbers can be
shown on a number line.

Example:

Add three and four.

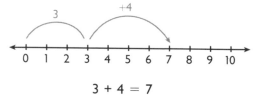

$3 + 4 = 7$

See operations, order

number machine

Number machines can carry out
operations such as addition,
subtraction, multiplication and
division. Calculators and
computers are types of number
machines.

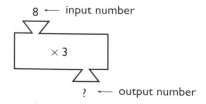

(1) The number 8 is put into the
machine. This is the **input**
number.
(2) The number is multiplied by
three. This is the **rule**.
(3) What comes out is the answer.

See calculator, rule

number pattern

See pattern

number sentence

A statement about numbers, usually in symbols rather than words.

Examples:

6 + 7 = 13	(true)
4 ≠ 9	(true)
5 + □ = 9	(open)
7 + 9 = 10	(false)
3 + 1 < 3 × 1	(false)

See open number sentence, symbol

number track

A track, as used in dice games, where the cells are numbered.

Example:

14	13	12	11	10	9	8	7	6	5	4
15	30	29	28	FORWARD TO 35		27	26	25	24	3
16	31	42	41	40	39	38	37	36	23	2
17	GO BACK TO 29	43	GO BACK TO 34		FINISH			35	GO BACK TO 29	1
GO BACK TO 9	GO BACK TO 29	32	GO BACK TO 23	33	34	FORWARD TO 41			START	
	18	19	FORWARD TO 30	20	GO BACK TO 13	21	22			

numeral

A symbol used to represent a number.

Example:

5 is the numeral which represents the number five.

5 apples

5 and V (Roman) are numerals for the number five.

See numeration, Roman numerals, symbol

numeration

A system of symbols used to represent numbers. Our system uses the symbols:
0, 1, 2, 3, 4, 5, 6, 7, 8 and 9.

See Hindu–Arabic, symbol

numerator

The top number in a fraction. It tells how many parts of the whole there are.

Example:

$$\frac{3}{4}$$ ← numerator
← denominator

In $\frac{3}{4}$ the numerator is 3.

Three out of four equal parts are coloured.

See denominator, fraction

162° obtuse angle

See angle, right angle, straight angle

oblique

A slanting line that is neither vertical nor horizontal.

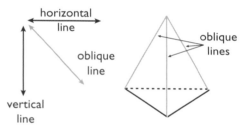

See askew

oblong

Another word for a rectangle or for rectangular.

oblong

See rectangle

obtuse angle

An angle bigger than a right angle (90°) but smaller than a straight angle (180°).

Examples:

obtuse angle

obtuse triangle

A triangle with one obtuse (larger than 90°) angle.

95°

120°

See acute triangle

o'clock

Used when telling time.

Example:

We say: six o'clock, ten o'clock ... only when talking about full hours.

Not used when telling hours and minutes: six fifteen, quarter to seven.

octagon

A plane shape (polygon) with eight sides and eight angles.

Examples: regular octagon

irregular octagons

See plane shape, polygon

octahedron

A solid (polyhedron) with eight faces.
A regular octahedron is formed by eight congruent equilateral triangles.

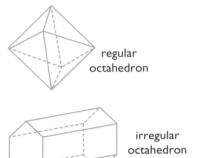

regular octahedron

irregular octahedron

See polyhedron, regular polyhedron

odd number

A number which, when divided by two, leaves a remainder of 1.
All odd numbers finish with one of the digits 1, 3, 5, 7 or 9.

See even number

one-dimensional

(1D)

A figure which has only length is said to be one-dimensional.

Examples:

A line has only length; therefore, it has only one dimension.

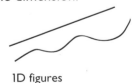

1D figures

See dimension, plane

one-to-one correspondence

A matching of the objects of two sets.

Examples:

Cups and saucers.
Straws and bottles.
Jumpers and children.

A correspondence between two sets for which each member of each set is paired with only one member of the other set. Arrows are used to show the corresponding objects.

SET A = (Jenny, Dad, Jim)

SET B = (fish,   pipe, fishing rod)

See arrow diagram, correspondence, many-to-one correspondence

open curve

A curve which has a beginning and an end which do not meet.

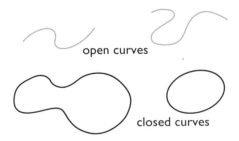

open curves

closed curves

See closed curve, curve

open number sentence

A mathematical sentence that contains numbers and variables. It can be an equation or an inequation.

Examples:

Equations	Inequations
$5 + \triangle = 10$	$4a \neq 9$
$3 \square - 1 = 25$	$5x - 5 < 33$
$\frac{x}{2} - 5 = 7$	$10 - y \geq 28$

See equation, inequality, inequation, number sentence

operation

There are four arithmetic operations:

		Examples:
Addition	+	$2 + 4$
Subtraction	−	$7 - 3$
Multiplication	×	10×5
Division	÷	$8 \div 4$

See addition, arithmetic, basic facts, division, multiplication, order of operations, subtraction

operators

The signs used in operations.

$$+ \quad - \quad \times \quad \div$$

Examples:

$10 + 2 \quad 7 \times 3 \quad 8 - 4 \quad 18 \div 6$

See operation

opposite numbers

Numbers that add up to zero.

Example:

$$-5 + 5 = 0$$

The opposite to −5 is 5; the opposite to 320 is −320.

order

(i) To order means to arrange in a pattern or a sequence.

(ii) Order means a pattern or a sequence.

(iii) Order of numbers on a number line.

See ascending, descending, number line, pattern, sequence

ordered pair

Two numbers (called x-coordinate and y-coordinate) written in a certain order.
Ordered pairs are usually written between brackets.

Example: (5, 3)

The x-coordinate is always written first. The ordered pair ■ (3, 5) is not the same as the ordered pair ● (5, 3).
The point marked 0 is the origin.

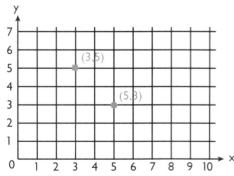

See axis, brackets, coordinates, origin

ordering

Placement according to size, colour, numerical value, etc.

Example:

order of operations

Used when evaluating complex number sentences.

(i) Number sentences with grouping symbols.

When grouping symbols are used, working is done from inside the brackets out.

Example:

$5 \{3 - [(4 \times 9) - (20 - 4)] + 19\}$

$= 5 \{3 - [36 - 16] + 19\}$

$= 5 \{3 - 20 + 19\}$

$= 5 \times 2$

$= 10$

(ii) When no grouping symbols are used, starting from the left do all multiplications and divisions, then again from the left, do all additions and subtractions.

Example:

$48 \div 3 + 2 - 4 \times 3$

$(48 \div 3) + 2 - (4 \times 3)$ insert brackets around multiplication and division

$= 16 + 2 - 12$ do addition first,
$= 18 - 12$ then subtraction

$= 6$

(iii) Sometimes 'of' is used.

Example:

$5 (3 + 8) - \frac{1}{2}$ of 10

$= 5 \times 11 - (\frac{1}{2} \times 10)$

$= 55 - 5$

$= 50$

Note: To remember the order of operations, do:
Brackets first, Of, Division, Multiplication, Addition, Subtraction.
Think : BODMAS.

See brackets, grouping symbols, operations

ordinal number

A number which indicates position.

Examples: 1st   2nd   3rd   4th

See cardinal number

origin

A point at which something begins.

Example:

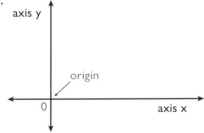

The coordinates of the origin are (0, 0).

The point where axes x and y intersect is called the origin and is marked 0.

See axis, coordinates, intersect, ordered pair

outcome

Result.

Example:

In tossing a coin, there are two possible outcomes, either heads or tails.

output

See number machine

oval

(i) An egg-shaped figure which is symmetrical about one axis. One end is more pointed than the other.

Example:

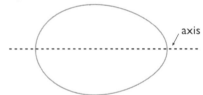

(ii) Another word for an ellipse, which is symmetrical about two axes.

Example:

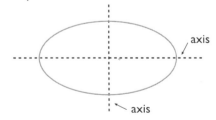

See axis, ellipse, symmetry

palindrome

A number or word that reads the same forward as backward.

Examples:
1991   19. 9. 1991   madam

pantograph

An instrument for tracing a drawing, map or a picture. Also used for the enlargement or reduction of an original.

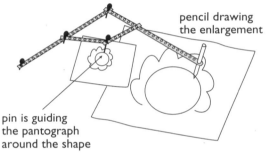

pencil drawing the enlargement

pin is guiding the pantograph around the shape

See enlargement

parallelepiped

A prism, made of parallelograms.

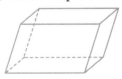

See parallelogram, prism

parallel lines
(Symbols: )

(i) Two or more lines that go in exactly the same direction. Parallel lines always remain the same distance apart. They never meet.

p.a.

Per annum. Per year.

Example:
The bank charges 7% interest p.a.

pace

The distance between your feet when you take a step. It is measured from heel to heel. It is used as an arbitrary unit for estimating distances.

My pace measures 55 centimetres

1 pace

See arbitrary unit, distance, estimate

pair

Two things that belong together.

Example:

a pair of socks

Examples:

train lines are parallel

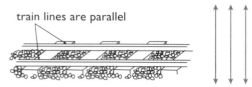

(ii) When parallel lines are crossed by a transversal, pairs of angles are formed. They have special properties:

1 corresponding angles
(make F-shape). They are equal.

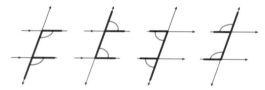

2 alternate angles
(make Z-shape). They are equal.

3 cointerior angles
(make U-shape). They add up to 180°.

 $a° + b° = 180°$

See transversal, vertically opposite

parallelogram

A four-sided figure (quadrilateral) in which both pairs of opposite sides are parallel and equal, and the opposite angles are equal.

Examples:

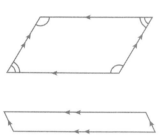

The arrow marks show which pairs of lines are parallel. A right-angled parallelogram is a rectangle.

Example:

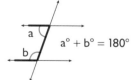

See parallel lines, quadrilateral, rectangle

parentheses

See brackets

partition

See division

Pascal's triangle

Used in probability.

```
            1
          1   1
        1   2   1
      1   3   3   1
    1   4   6   4   1
  1   5  10  10   5   1
1   6  15  20  15   6   1
1  7  21  35  35  21  7  1
```

Notice that after the second line the new numbers are made by adding the numbers in the previous line.

path

A connected set of points.
The route or line along which a person or object moves.

Example:

The path of my hop-step-jump

pattern

A repeated design or arrangement using shapes, lines, colours, numbers, etc.

Examples:
(i) Shape pattern

(ii) Colour pattern

(iii) A 'number pattern' is a sequence of numbers formed by following a 'rule'.

Examples:
1, 4, 7, 10 … (rule: add three)

$16, 8, 4, 2, 1, \frac{1}{2}, \frac{1}{4}, \frac{1}{8}$ …
(rule: divide by two)

See rule, sequence

pattern blocks

Sets of plastic, wood or cardboard shapes in the form of triangles, squares, parallelograms, hexagons, etc.

Examples:

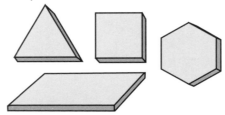

pegboard

Plastic or wooden board containing holes in which pegs can be placed.

Example:

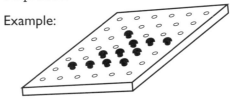

Coloured pegs are used to represent numbers, patterns or shapes.

pendulum

A small heavy object attached to a string suspended from a fixed point.

Example:

object

If the string is one metre in length, then it takes about one second to make a single complete swing, over and back.

See second

pentagon

A shape (polygon) with five straight sides and five angles.

Examples:

irregular pentagon   regular pentagon

See polygon

per cent (percentage)

(Symbol: %)

A number out of one hundred.

Example:

This is a 'hundred square'. Fifteen out of the hundred little squares have been coloured in. They represent:

$$\frac{15}{100} = 15\% = 0.15$$

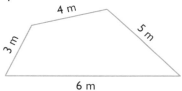

fraction   percentage   decimal fraction

See decimal fraction, fraction

perimeter

The distance around a closed shape, or the length of its boundary.

Example:

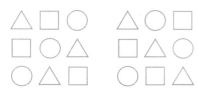

To find the perimeter of a shape, add the lengths of all its sides.
The perimeter is:

$$3 m + 4 m + 5 m + 6 m = 18 m$$

See boundary, circumference

permutation

An ordered arrangement or sequence of a group of objects.

Example:
Three shapes ○ △ □ can be arranged in six different ways, or have six permutations.

△□○   △○□

□○△   □△○

○△□   ○□△

The order in which the shapes are arranged is important in a permutation. When the order is not important, the arrangement is called a combination.

See combination

perpendicular

Forming a right angle.

(i) Perpendicular height

   The line segment drawn from the vertex (top) of a figure to the opposite side at a 90° angle.

Examples:

The height of a triangle, cone or pyramid

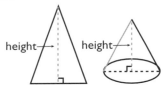

(ii) Perpendicular lines

   Lines which intersect to make right angles.

Examples:

See altitude, apex, cone, line segment, pyramid, triangle, vertex

perspective

When drawing on paper, we can show depth by drawing all parallel lines running into one or several points on the horizon. These points are called vanishing points. The drawing looks like it is three-dimensional. We say it has perspective.

See converging lines

pi
(Symbol: π)

The ratio of the circumference of a circle to its diameter.

$$\pi = \frac{\text{circumference}}{\text{diameter}}$$

The approximate value of π is 3.14. The exact value cannot be worked out.

See chronological order, circle, circumference, diameter, radius

pictograph

(pictogram)

A graph drawn with pictures that represent the real objects.

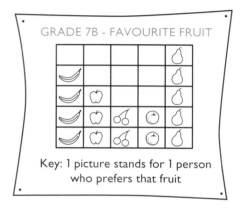

A pictograph must have a heading and a key.

See graph

picture graph

Another name for pictograph.

pie graph

(pie chart)

A circle graph.

Example:

How Linda spends a day.

See graph

place holder

(i) A symbol which holds the place for an unknown number.

Examples:

In $w + 3 = 7$, w is the place holder.
In $\square - 6 = 10$, $\square$ is the place holder.

(ii) Zero, when used with other digits, is used as a place holder.

Example: 6800

The zero in place of units and tens helps us to see that the numeral 8 means eight hundreds, the numeral 6 means six thousand and that there are no units and no tens.

See digit, equation, variable

place value

The value of each digit in a number depends on its place or position in that number.

Examples:

hundreds	tens	units
4	8	6
	1	8
8	2	3

In the number 486 the value of digit 8 is 80 (eight tens).

In the number 18 the value of digit 8 is 8 (eight units).

In the number 823 the value of digit 8 is 800 (eight hundreds).

See decimal place-value system, digit, value

plan

(i)   To prepare ahead of time.

Example: Plan for a holiday.

(ii) A diagram of an object as seen from above.

Example:

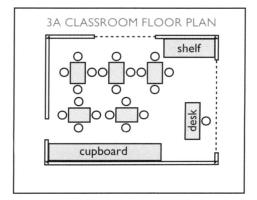

A floor plan of a classroom

See cross-section, diagram, front view, side view

planar figure

A two-dimensional shape, such as a triangle. Also called a plane figure or plane shape.

Examples:

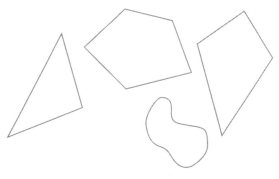

See plane shape, triangle, two-dimensional

plane

A flat surface, like the floor of a house or a wall.

A plane extends infinitely in all directions.

Two-dimensional objects are called plane shapes or planar figures because they can be drawn in one plane.

Example:

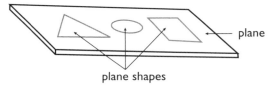

plane shapes

See dimension, infinite, planar figure, two-dimensional

plane shape

A plane shape is a closed shape that can be drawn on a flat surface.

Examples:

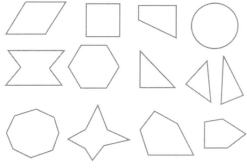

See non-planar figure, planar figure

platonic solids

See regular polyhedron

plus

(Symbol: +)

The name of the symbol that means addition.

Example:

$$4 + 6 = 10$$

See addition

p.m.

(post meridiem)

The time from immediately after midday until immediately before midnight.
p.m. is used only with 12-hour time.

Example:

It is evening.
The time is half past seven.
It is 7:30 p.m.

See a.m.

point

(i) Small dot on a surface. It has no dimension.

. P

The dot shows where the point P is.

(ii) The dot, called the decimal point, shows that 4 means four dollars and 50 is fifty cents.

$4 50

See decimal point

polygon

A plane shape which has three or more straight sides; for example, a triangle, quadrilateral, pentagon or hexagon.

Examples:

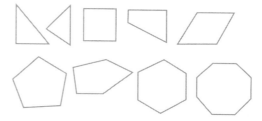

See closed shape, hexagon, irregular polygon, line segment, octagon, pentagon, quadrilateral, regular polygon, triangle

polyhedron

(Plural: polyhedrons or polyhedra)

A three-dimensional shape with plane faces.

Examples:

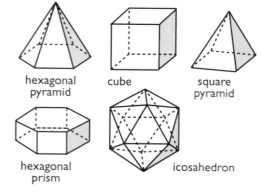

hexagonal pyramid   cube   square pyramid

hexagonal prism   icosahedron

See cube, dodecahedron, icosahedron, prism, pyramid, regular polyhedron

polyomino

A plane shape made of squares of the same size, each square being connected to at least one of the others by a common edge.

Examples:

domino – two squares

triomino – three squares

tetromino – four squares

pentomino – five squares

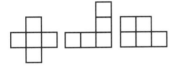

See planar figure

position

Describes the place where something is.

Examples:

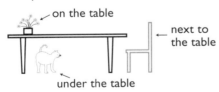

On, under, above, behind, in front of, between, next to, outside, etc.

See coordinates, ordered pairs

positive numbers

Numbers greater than zero. We sometimes write the plus sign (+) in front of them.

Examples:

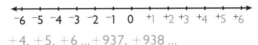

+4, +5, +6 ... +937, +938 ...

See integers, negative numbers, plus, zero

power of a number

In 2^4 the power is 4.
It means $2 \times 2 \times 2 \times 2 = 16$
Say: two to the power of four.
When the power is zero, the value is one.

$$10^0 = 1 \qquad\qquad 1000^0 = 1$$

See cubed number, index, index notation, square number, zero power

prediction

In mathematics we can predict or estimate possible answers.

See estimate, probability

prefix

A word before a unit, showing us how large the measure is.

Example:

One millimetre means one thousandth of a metre.

See Prefixes tables on pages 155–6

prime factor of a number

A prime number that will divide exactly into a given number.

Example:

2, 3 and 5 are the prime factors of thirty. (10 is a factor of thirty, but not a prime factor.)

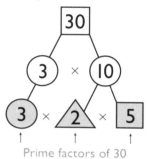

Prime factors of 30

See factor tree, factors, prime number

prime number

A counting number that can only be divided by one and itself.

Examples:

2, 3, 5, 7, 11, 13, 17 ...
The factors of two are 2 and 1.
The factors of five are 5 and 1.

A prime number has only two factors, itself and 1.

Note: Number 1 is usually considered to be neither prime nor composite.

See composite number, counting number, factor

prism

A solid figure with two faces that are parallel and the same in size and shape. They can be any polygon.

Examples:

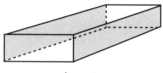

rectangular prism

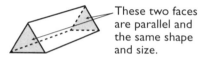

These two faces are parallel and the same shape and size.

triangular prism

All cuboids are prisms.

See cuboid, face, parallel, polygon, polyhedron, prism, three-dimensional

probability

The likelihood of an event happening.

Example:

If a coin is tossed, the probability of getting tails is $\frac{1}{2}$.

See chance event, equally likely

problem solving

Using your understanding and knowledge of mathematical concepts and principles to find a solution in a new or unfamiliar situation.

product

The answer to a multiplication problem.

Example:

$$3 \times 2 = 6$$

multiplicand   multiplier   product

Six is the product.

See associative property of multiplication, commutative property of multiplication, multiplicand, multiplication, multiplier

progression

A sequence of numbers following a given rule. The numbers in a progression increase or decrease in a constant way.

(i) If the rule is 'add a number', it is called an **arithmetic progression**.

Examples:
Rule: add 3   1, 4, 7, 10, 13, 16, ...
Rule: subtract 2   21, 19, 17, 15, 13, 11, ...

(ii) If the rule is 'multiply by a number', it is called a **geometric progression**.

Examples:
Rule: multiply by 4   1, 4, 16, 64, 256, ...
Rule: divide by 2   12, 6, 3, 1.5, 0.75, ...

See decrease, increase, sequence

projection

The transformation of one shape or picture to another.

Example:

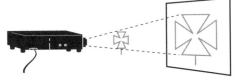

Projecting a picture on a screen.

See transformation

pronumeral

Another word for the symbol representing an unknown value in an equation. The pronumeral stands for a particular value.

Examples:
$2a = 6$ $7 - x = 5$ $12 \times \square = 24$
$a = 3$ $x = 2$ $\square = 2$

a, x and □ are pronumerals.

See algebraic expression, symbol, variable

proper fraction

A fraction where the numerator is less than the denominator.

Examples:

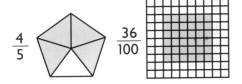

$\frac{4}{5}$ $\frac{36}{100}$

See denominator, fraction, improper fraction, numerator, simple fraction

property

A characteristic of an object.

See attribute, classification, classify

proportion

A statement of equality between two ratios.

1   Direct proportion

When a relation between two variables remains constant, they are said to be in direct proportion.

Example:

Mary reads three pages of a book every ten minutes.

The ratio $\frac{pages}{time}$ is constant.

$$\frac{3\ pages}{10\ min} = \frac{6\ pages}{20\ min} = \frac{9\ pages}{30\ min} = \frac{12\ pages}{40\ min} \cdots$$

2   Indirect (or inverse) proportion

When one variable is multiplied by a number and the other variable is divided by the same number, they are said to be in indirect proportion.

Example:

It takes four hours for one person to mow the lawn.

It takes two hours for two people to mow the lawn.

Number of people	1	2	3	4	8
Time in hours	4	2	$1\frac{1}{3}$	1	$\frac{1}{2}$

See inverse proportion, ratio, variable

protractor

An instrument used to measure and draw angles.

pyramid

A solid (3D shape) which has a polygon for a base and all the other faces are triangles.

Example:

This pyramid has a square base and the other faces are congruent triangles.

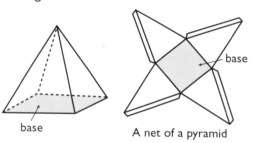

base

A net of a pyramid

A tetrahedron is a pyramid with a triangular base.

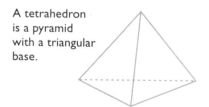

The base of a pyramid can be any polygon.

See apex, base, face, isosceles triangle, net, polygon, solid, tetrahedron, vertex

Pythagoras' theorem

In any right-angled triangle, the square of the hypotenuse is equal to the sum of the squares of the sides.

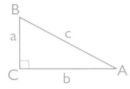

$$c^2 = a^2 + b^2$$
$$a^2 = c^2 - b^2$$
$$b^2 = c^2 - a^2$$

Example:

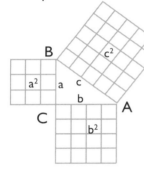

$$c^2 = a^2 + b^2$$
$$5^2 = 3^2 + 4^2$$
$$25 = 9 + 16$$
$$25 = 25$$

$$a = \sqrt{c^2 - b^2}$$
$$b = \sqrt{c^2 - a^2}$$
$$c = \sqrt{a^2 + b^2}$$

quadrant

(i)   A quarter of the circumference of a circle.

quadrilateral

A plane shape with four sides and four angles.

Example:

Some special quadrilaterals are:

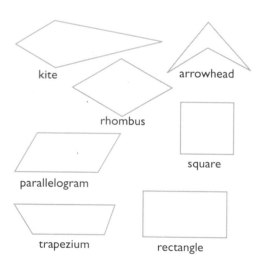

kite

arrowhead

rhombus

square

parallelogram

trapezium

rectangle

See kite, parallelogram, planar figure, rectangle, rhombus, square, trapezium

(ii) A plane figure made by two radii of a circle at a 90° angle and the arc cut off by them.

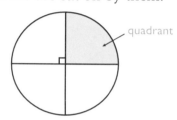

quadrant

(iii) In coordinate geometry we use the space between the axis-x and axis-y. We can extend the x-axis and the y-axis so that all four quadrants of the number plane can be seen. Quadrants are numbered in an anticlockwise direction.

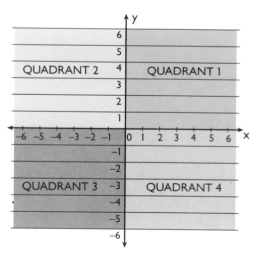

See arc, coordinates, ordered pair, radius

quadruple

Increase the amount four times.

Example:
quadruple $20 means
4 × $20 = $80

See double, treble

quantity

The amount or number
of something.

Example:

The quantity of
lemonade in a bottle is one litre.

quarter

One of four equal parts.

Examples:

$\frac{1}{4}$ is shaded

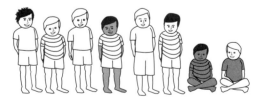

quarter of the boys are sitting

quotient

The answer to a division problem.

Example:

$$10 \div 2 = 5$$

dividend   divisor   quotient

Five is the quotient.

See dividend, division, divisor

quotition

See division

radian

The radian is the angle at the centre of a circle (approximately 57.3°), when the length of the arc is equal to the radius.

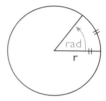

See arc, radius

radiant point

A point from which rays or radii start.

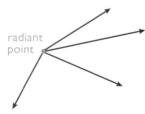

See ray

radius of a circle

(Plural: radii)

(i) The distance from the centre of a circle to its circumference (or from the centre to the surface of a sphere).

Example:

(ii) The line segment joining the centre and a point of the circle (like the spoke of a wheel) or a line segment joining the centre of a sphere to a point on its surface.

See circle, circumference, diameter, line segment, sphere

random sample

A term in statistics meaning a part or portion which is chosen to represent the whole.

Example:

A bag with twenty black and twenty white balls. A random sample may be three white and two black balls.

See statistics

rate

(i) The comparison between two quantities, which may be of different things.

Example:
Sixty kilometres per hour (60 km/h) is the rate of travel.

(ii) The exchange rate is the comparison of values of money.

Example:
US$1 = A$0.67

See comparison

ratio

(Symbol: :)

A comparison of two quantities. We express one quantity as a fraction of the other.

Example:

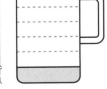

5 parts water

1 part cordial

To make a jug of cordial, mix the cordial and water in the ratio of 1:5. This means that you mix one part of cordial to five parts of water.

The order of the numbers is important: 1:5 ≠ 5:1.

See comparison

rational number

A number that can be expressed as a fraction or ratio of integers.

Examples:

$$\frac{3}{4} \qquad 0.5 = \frac{1}{2} \qquad 8 = \frac{8}{1}$$

All rational numbers can be represented by either:

1   Decimal numbers that terminate.

Examples:

$$\frac{3}{4} = 0.75 \qquad \frac{1}{8} = 0.125$$

2   Non-terminating, repeating decimals.

Examples:

$$\frac{2}{3} = 0.6\dot{6} \qquad \frac{-4}{11} = -0.\dot{3}\dot{6}$$

See fraction, ratio, recurring decimal

ray

A half line. It has a starting point but no end. It extends in one direction only.

Examples:

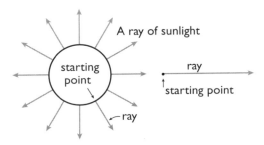

A ray of sunlight

starting point

ray

starting point

ray

See angle, line, line segment, radiant point

reciprocal

The reciprocal of a fraction is the fraction obtained by interchanging the numerator and denominator.

Example:

Reciprocal?
Turn the fraction
upside down

(i) Since we can write 4 as $\frac{4}{1}$ the reciprocal of 4 is $\frac{1}{4}$.

(ii) Reciprocal of $\frac{2}{3}$ is $\frac{3}{2}$ or $1\frac{1}{2}$.

rectangle

A quadrilateral with two pairs of equal and parallel sides, and four right angles.

Example:

A rectangle is sometimes called an oblong.

See parallel, quadrilateral, right angle

rectangular numbers

Numbers that can be represented by dots arranged in a rectangle.

Examples:

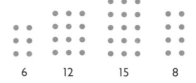

| 6 | 12 | 15 | 8 |

rectangular prism

A polyhedron whose base is a rectangle. Another name for a cuboid.

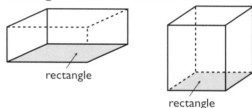

rectangle

rectangle

Most boxes are rectangular prisms.

See cuboid

recurring decimal

A decimal fraction in which one or more digits are repeated indefinitely.

Examples:

(i) $\frac{1}{3} = 0.33333... = 0.\dot{3}$

It is written $0.\dot{3}$. The dot shows that the digit is repeated.

(ii) $0.\dot{1}\dot{7}$

These dots show that the digits 1 and 7 are repeated.

0.171 717 171 7...

(iii) $\frac{1}{7} = 0.142\ 857\ 142\ 857\ ...$

It is written either as $0.\dot{1}42\ 85\dot{7}$ or $0.\overline{142857}$ to show the repeated digits.

See decimal fraction, digit, rational number, terminating decimal

reduce

(i) Simplify. Express a fraction in its simplest form.

Example:

$\frac{5}{30}$ can be reduced to $\frac{1}{6}$

(ii) Make smaller.

See cancelling, enlargement, fraction, transformation

reflection

Being reflected. Reflecting.

Examples:

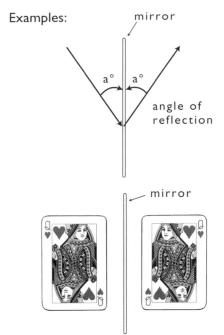

See flip, mirror image

reflex angle

An angle greater than a straight angle (180°) but less than a revolution (360°).

Examples:

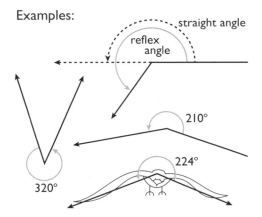

See angle, revolution, straight angle

region

(i) Plane region.

All the points inside a simple closed shape together with all of the points on the boundary of the shape.

(ii) Solid region.

All the points inside a closed surface together with all the points on the surface.

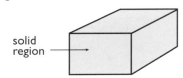

See boundary, plane, solid, surface

regroup

Exchange.

Examples:

(i) Twelve unit blocks can be regrouped (exchanged) for one long (10) and two units.

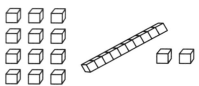

(ii) Before subtracting fifteen, the eight tens and two units have been regrouped into seven tens and twelve units.

$$\begin{array}{r} 7\ 12 \\ 8\,\overset{}{2} \\ -15 \\ \hline 67 \end{array}$$

See carrying, group, multibase arithmetic blocks (MAB)

regular polygon

A polygon is regular if its sides are equal in length and its angles are equal in size.

Some common regular polygons are:

Equilateral triangle	three sides
Square	four sides
Regular pentagon	five sides
Regular hexagon	six sides

equilateral triangle   square

regular pentagon   regular hexagon

See equilateral triangle, hexagon, irregular polygon, pentagon

regular polyhedron

A polyhedron whose faces are congruent regular polygons, that are exactly the same in shape and size. Internal angles are also the same in size. Regular polyhedrons are also called platonic solids.

There are only five regular polyhedrons:

tetrahedron   hexahedron (cube)   dodecahedron

octahedron   icosahedron

See congruent, dodecahedron, face, hexahedron, icosahedron, octahedron, polyhedron, tetrahedron

regular shape

See regular polygon

relation

Connection, correspondence or contrast between a pair of objects, measures, numbers, etc. Also called relationship.

Examples:

(i) Family relationship: Judi is the sister of Lea.

(ii) Size relation: Jan is taller than Helen.

(iii) Mathematical relation.

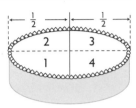

2 is half of 4

(iv) Relation between pairs of numbers. Often presented in a table.

×	1	2	3	4	5
y	6	7	8	9	10

$$y = x + 5$$

See arrow diagram, correspondence

remainder

The amount left over after division.

Example:
There are different ways of expressing the remainder in the answer. They depend on the question.

$$\begin{array}{r} 25 \\ 5\overline{)128} \\ 28 \\ 3 \end{array}$$

remainder

Examples:
(i) Question: Five boys share 128 marbles. How many marbles each?

Answer: Each boy gets 25 marbles. 3 marbles are left over.

(ii) Question: Share $128 among five girls.

Answer: Each girl gets $25 and $\frac{3}{5}$ of a dollar; that is, $25 and 60c.

See division

rename

Change expression.

Examples:
(i) Rename kilograms into grams.
$1\frac{3}{4}$ kg = 1750 g = 1.75 kg
(ii) Rename fraction.
$\frac{7}{3} = 2\frac{1}{3}$

repeating decimal

See recurring decimal

reverse

The other way round, or opposite way round.

Example:
The reverse of 385 is 583.

reverse operation

Multiplication is the reverse of division.
Addition is the reverse of subtraction.

See inverse of an operation, operation

revolution

One complete turn. There are 360° in one revolution.
There are four right angles in one revolution.

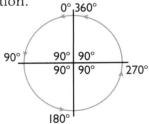

See angle, right angle

rhombus

A shape (parallelogram) with four equal sides. Opposite angles are equal.

Examples:

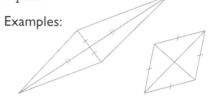

See diamond, parallelogram

right angle

(Symbol: ⌐)

An angle measuring exactly 90°.

Examples:

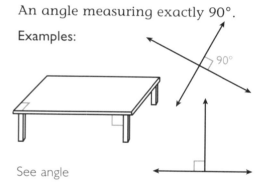

See angle

right-angled triangle

A triangle with a right angle.

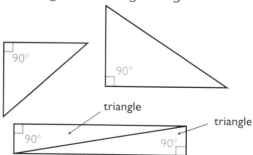

See Pythagoras' theorem, right angle

right 3D shape

A solid with ends or base perpendicular to height.

Examples:

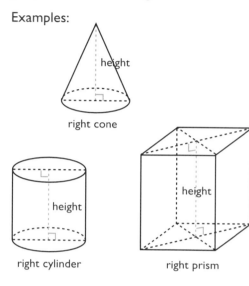

right cone

right cylinder   right prism

See cone, cylinder, prism

rigid

Not flexible. Stiff. A jointed structure is rigid when its angles cannot be changed (the struts will not move out of place).
A triangle forms a rigid structure.

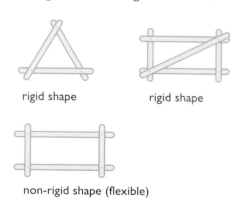

rigid shape   rigid shape

non-rigid shape (flexible)

See flexible

Roman numerals

An ancient system of numeration, where the numbers are represented by letters of the Roman alphabet.

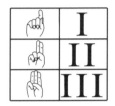 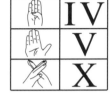

The numerals are made up of a combination of these symbols.

I	(1)	C	(100) centum
V	(5)	D	(500)
X	(10)	M	(1000) mille
L	(50)		

Examples:

2000 — MM
2002 — MMII

See numeration, Useful Information
page 150

rotate

Move around an axis or centre. Revolve. Turn round and round.

Examples:

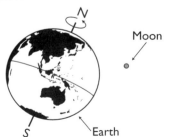

The Earth rotates around its axis.
The Moon revolves around the earth.

rotation

The process by which an object changes position by turning about a fixed point through a given angle.

Examples:

quarter turn
(a rotation through 90°)

half turn
(a rotation through 180°)

three-quarter turn
(a rotation through 270°)

rotational symmetry

When a shape is turned through an angle less than 360° and remains the same, it has rotational symmetry.

Example:

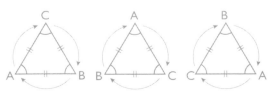

Equilateral triangle has rotational symmetry

rounding

1 Writing an answer to a given degree of accuracy.

Example:

2764 rounded to the nearest ten becomes 2760

rounded to the nearest hundred becomes 2800

rounded to the nearest thousand becomes 3000

2 Numbers ending in 1, 2, 3 and 4, round down to the lower number.

Examples:

54 rounded to the nearest ten becomes 50.

348 rounded to the nearest hundred becomes 300.

3 Numbers ending in 5, 6, 7, 8 and 9 round up to the higher number.

Examples:

55 rounded to the nearest 10 becomes 60.

356 rounded to the nearest 100 becomes 400.

See accurate, estimate, significant figures

route

A path. A way taken from start to finish, which may be traversed.

Example:

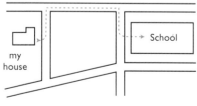

My route to school

row

(i) A horizontal arrangement.

Example:

3 rows of pears

(ii) Things arranged so that they make a line going from left to right.

Examples:

A row of numbers: 4, 5, 6, 7, 8, 9, ...

A row of seats in the theatre

See column, horizontal

rule

(i) An instruction to do something in a particular way.

Example:

Find the rule for this sequence.

1, 4, 7, 10, 13

+3 +3 +3 +3

The rule is 'add 3'.

(ii) Numbers in a relation are following a rule.

Example:

t	1	2	3	4	5	6
D	15	30	45	60	75	90

The rule is $D = 15t$

(iii) To draw a line using a ruler.

See cycle game, number machine, progression, sequence

....

ruler

An instrument for drawing straight lines, usually made of plastic or wood. It has a scale for measuring length.

See graduated, scale

s

Symbol for second.

same

Identical, alike, unchanged, not different.

Example:

See congruent   same shapes

sample

A selection of a few items taken from a larger set.

Example:

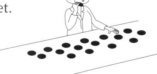

In a biscuit factory they take a sample of each batch of biscuits.

satisfy

In mathematics it means 'make the equation true'.

Example:

If $x < 5$, which of the numbers 8, 3, 35 or 4 satisfy the inequation?

Answer: 3 and 4, because $3 < 5$ and $4 < 5$.

scale

(i) A thermometer, a ruler or a balance has a scale marked on it to measure temperature, length and mass.

Examples:

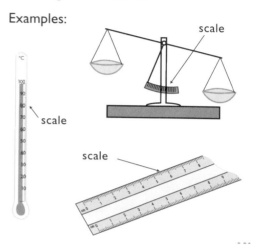

(ii) A number line used on a graph.

Example:

(iii) The scale on a map or a plan shows the ratio for making things larger or smaller.

Example:

SCALE OF KILOMETRES

1 cm = 10 km

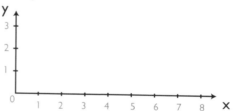

1 : 1 000 000

See balance, enlarge, graph, number line, reduce, ruler, thermometer

scale drawing

A drawing or plan on which the real object is made bigger or smaller while keeping the same proportions.

Example:

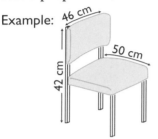

The child's chair was made similar to the adult's chair on a scale 1 to 2 or 1 : 2.

See proportion

scalene triangle

A triangle with each side different in length.

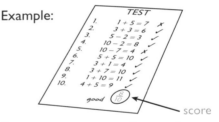

See right 3D shape, triangle

scales

Instruments used for finding or comparing weights or masses.

Examples:

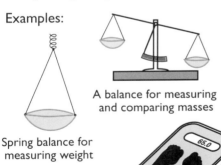

Spring balance for measuring weight

A balance for measuring and comparing masses

Bathroom scales

A balance for comparing masses

See mass, weight

scientific notation

A shorthand way of writing very large or very small numbers using powers of ten.

Example:

(i) 6 300 000 = 6.3 × 1 000 000

$= 6.3 \times 10^6$

6 places

(ii) 0.000 567 = 5.67 × 0.000 1

$= 5.67 \times 10^{-4}$

4 places

See expanded notation, index notation

score

The amount of points or marks gained in a competition or test.

Example:

score

See average, mean, median, mode

second

(i) second (2nd): The ordinal number which comes after first (1st) and before third (3rd).

1st   2nd   3rd

See ordinal number

(ii) second (symbol: s): A measurement of time. There are sixty seconds in one minute.

Example:

One second is the time taken by a pendulum about one metre long to make one complete swing, over and back.

See pendulum

(iii) second in angle measurement (symbol: ″)

See degree

section

(i) A flat surface obtained by cutting through a solid in any direction.

Example:

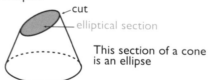

This section of a cone is an ellipse

(ii) When the cut is parallel to the base of the solid, it is called a cross-section.

Example:

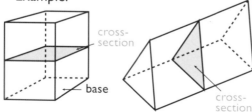

See cone, cross-section, ellipse, flat, frustum, segment, solid, surface

segment

A part, a section of something.

Examples:
(i) A line segment.

A   line segment   B

(ii) A segment of a circle is the part of the circle between an arc and its chord.

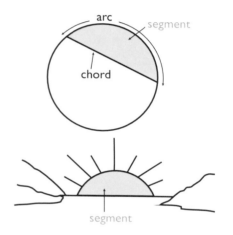

See arc, chord

semicircle

Half a circle.
When you cut a circle along its diameter, you get two semicircles.

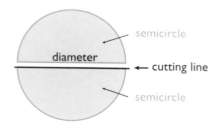

See circle, diameter

sentence

A statement. In mathematics a sentence may contain pronumerals, numerals and other symbols.

See false sentence, number sentence, numeral, open sentence, pronumeral, symbol, true sentence

sequence

A pattern, following an order or rule.

Examples:

(i) 1, 3, 5, 7, ...

The rule of this sequence is 'add 2'.

(ii)

In this sequence each shape is following a pattern of rotation anticlockwise by the same amount of turn.

See anticlockwise, order, pattern, progression, rotation, rule

seriate

To put in order.

Example:

These sticks are seriated according to length.

set

(Symbol: { })

A group of objects or numbers. Each object in a set is called a member or an element of the set. The elements of a set are written inside braces { }.

Example:
Set of whole numbers = $\{0, 1, 2, 3, 4 \ldots\}$

See braces, cardinal number, element of a set, subset, whole number

set square

An instrument used for geometrical drawings, made of wood, plastic or metal.

Examples:

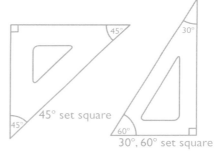

45° set square

30°, 60° set square

Set squares are used for drawing parallel lines, right and other angles, etc.

See parallel lines, right angle

shadow stick measuring

A useful, old method for calculating heights that cannot be directly measured. It is based on the properties of similar triangles.

Example:

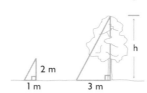

sun

$$\frac{h}{3} = \frac{2}{1}$$

$$h = 6 \text{ m}$$

We measure the shadow of a stick of a known length and the shadow cast by the tall object. The length of the stick and the object, and their shadows, are in the same ratio.

See ratio, similar

shape

The form of an object.

Examples:

2D shapes: triangles, quadrilaterals
3D shapes: cubes, prisms, pyramids

See cube, dimension, prism, pyramid, quadrilateral, three-dimensional, triangle, two-dimensional

sharing

See division

SI

The International metric system. The symbol SI comes from the initials of the French term *Système Internationale d'Unités* (international unit system).
This system is based on the metre, gram, second, ampere, kelvin, candela and mole.

See metric system

side

A line segment which is a part of a perimeter or of a figure.

Example:

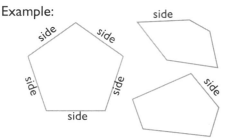

A pentagon has five sides.

See line segment, pentagon, perimeter

side view

A diagram, as seen from the side.

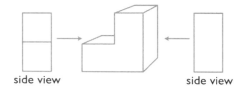

side view   side view

See cross-section, front view, plan

sign

A symbol used to show an operation or a statement.

Examples:

Addition sign	$+$
Subtraction sign	$-$
Multiplication sign	$\times$
Division signs	$\div$ ⟩ ⎴
Equal sign	$=$

See operation, symbol and the list of symbols on page 149

significant figure

A digit in a number that is considered important when rounding off or making an approximation.

Examples:

3745 rounded to two significant figures is 3700.

0.165 of a metre rounded to one significant figure is 0.2 of a metre.

See approximate, rounding

---

similar

The same in shape but not in size. Two shapes are similar if the corresponding angles are equal and all sides are enlarged or reduced in the same ratio.

Examples:

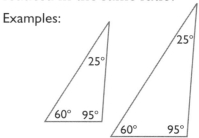

Similar triangles

See congruent, enlarge, ratio, reduce

---

simple fraction

A fraction such as $\frac{3}{4}, \frac{1}{2}, \frac{7}{10}$. Also called a common, proper or vulgar fraction.

Example:

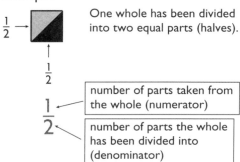

$\frac{1}{2} \rightarrow$ One whole has been divided into two equal parts (halves).

$\frac{1}{2}$

$1 \leftarrow$ number of parts taken from the whole (numerator)

$\overline{2} \leftarrow$ number of parts the whole has been divided into (denominator)

See denominator, fraction, numerator

---

simplify

Make simple. Write in the shortest, simplest form.

Example:

Simplify $\frac{8}{10} + \frac{4}{20}$

$= \frac{4}{5} + \frac{1}{5}$

$= \frac{5}{5}$

$= 1$

Simplify $\frac{a^2b}{ab}$

$= \frac{a \times \cancel{a}^1 \times \cancel{b}^1}{\cancel{a}_1 \times \cancel{b}_1}$

$= a$

See cancelling

---

simultaneous equations

Equations that have the same unknown quantities and are solved together.

Example:

$a + b = 10$
$2a = 6 \qquad \Rightarrow \quad \underline{a = 3} ✔$

$\overline{}$

$3 + b = 10$
$b = 10 - 3$
$\underline{b = 7} ✔$

Check:
$a + b = 10$
$3 + 7 = 10 ✔$

The solution is a = 3 and b = 7.

---

size

The amount, magnitude or dimension.

Examples:

(i) The size of this angle is 37°.

(ii) Helen wears size ten clothes and size two shoes.

skew lines

Lines that do not lie in the same plane; they cannot intersect and are not parallel.

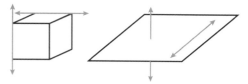

See intersect, parallel lines

slide

Change position on the surface.

See flip, rotation, translation, turn

solid

A solid is a figure with three dimensions, usually length, width and height (depth).

Examples:

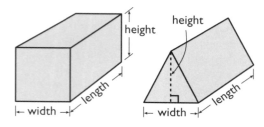

See height, length, three-dimensional, width

solution

The answer to a problem or question.

Example:

The equation $x + 4 = 9$
has a solution $x = 5$.

solve

Find the answer.

See calculate, solution

some

Not all of the whole. At least one.

Examples:

(i)

A whole cake   Some of the cake

(ii) Some of the children are walking away.

sorting

Putting objects into groups according to attributes.

Example:

Attributes are colour and thickness.

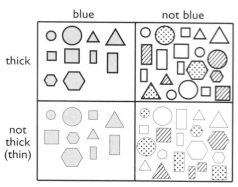

See attribute, Carroll diagram, classification, classify, group

space

Space is a three-dimensional region. Spatial figures (solids) have three dimensions.

See dimension, region, solid, three-dimensional

span

Stretch from side to side, across.

See handspan

spatial

Things which are relating to, or happening in, space.

speed

The rate of time at which something travels. The distance travelled in a unit of time.

Example:

A car travelled sixty kilometres in one hour. Its speed was **60 km/h**.

See distance, unit of measurement

sphere

A three-dimensional shape like a round ball. A sphere has one curved surface and no corners or edges. Every point on the sphere's surface is the same distance from the sphere's centre.

Examples:

A basketball   The Earth

See three-dimensional

spinner

A disc marked with numbers used in chance games.

Examples:

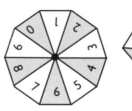 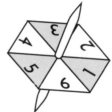

spiral

A curve like a coil on a flat surface.

Example:

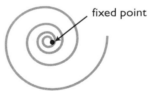

fixed point

A spiral is a continuous curve moving around a fixed point so that its distance from the fixed point is always increasing.

See curve, distance

spring balance

An instrument that measures weight. A spring inside it is extended by the force equal to the mass of the object.

See mass, weight

square

A quadrilateral with four equal sides and four right angles.

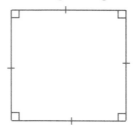

See quadrilateral, right angle

square centimetre

(Symbol: cm²)

A square centimetre is a unit for measuring area.

Examples:

1 cm

1 cm

The area is one square centimetre.

1 cm

3 cm

The area of this shape is three square centimetres.

$$3 \text{ cm} \times 1 \text{ cm} = 3 \text{ cm}^2$$

See area, unit of measurement

square kilometre

(Symbol: km²)

A unit for measuring very large areas.

$$1 \text{ km}^2 = 1\ 000\ 000 \text{ m}^2$$

Examples:
The area of the Northern Territory is 1 346 200 km².

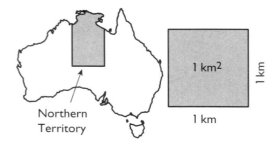

1 km²

1 km

1 km

Northern Territory

Smaller areas, like the sizes of towns or suburbs, are measured in hectares.

$$1 \text{ km}^2 = 100 \text{ ha}$$

See area, hectare, unit of measurement

square metre

(Symbol: m²)

A unit for measuring area.

$$1 \text{ m}^2 = 10\ 000 \text{ cm}^2$$

Examples:

(i) This man is holding a piece of cardboard which has an area of one square metre.

1 m

1 m

(ii) This rug has an area of 4.5 m².

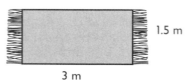

1.5 m

3 m

See area, square centimetre, unit of measurement

square number

A number that can be represented by dots in the shape of a square.

Examples:

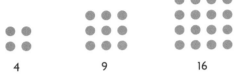

4   9   16

See index, index notation, triangle number

square of a number

The answer you get when you multiply a number by itself.

Examples:

$2^2 = 2 \times 2 = 4$

$3^2 = 3 \times 3 = 9$

$(0.5)^2 = 0.5 \times 0.5 = 0.25$

See index, index laws, square root

square paper

Paper ruled in squares, used for scale drawing and graphing.

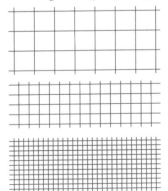

See scale drawing, graph, isometric paper

square root

A number which, when multiplied by itself, produces the given number. An inverse operation of squaring a number.

Examples:

$\sqrt{2} \times \sqrt{2} = 2$

$\sqrt{9} \times \sqrt{9} = 9$

$^+2^2 = 2 \times 2 = {}^+4$

$(^-2)^2 = {}^-2 \times {}^-2 = {}^+4$ $\Bigg\} \therefore \sqrt{4} = {}^\pm 2$

See square of a number

standard

Units of measure that are accepted by agreement are said to be 'standard measures'; for example, the metric measures.

See basic, SI, unit, unit of measurement

statistics

The study concerned with the collection and classification of numerical facts. The information collected is called data. Data can be represented in a table or on a graph, and interpreted and analysed.

Example: FAVOURITE FOODS

Meat	Vegetables	Fruit	Sweets
Paul S.	Carlo	Anne	Dean
John	Hirani	James	Belinda
Tibor		Paul B.	Quong
Jackie		Claire	Brad
Toula		Ranjit	Ali
Sarah			Anna
David			Jhiro
Jeremy			Peter
			Samantha
			Halima

The information in the table is the data. There are 25 children in the class.

8 children prefer meat

$$\therefore \quad \frac{8}{25} \times \frac{100}{1} = 32\% \text{ of the class prefer meat}$$

2 children prefer vegetables

$$\therefore \quad \frac{2}{25} \times \frac{100}{1} = 8\% \text{ of the class prefer vegetables}$$

5 children prefer fruit

$$\therefore \quad \frac{5}{25} \times \frac{100}{1} = 20\% \text{ of the class prefer fruit}$$

10 children prefer sweets

$$\therefore \quad \frac{10}{25} \times \frac{100}{1} = 40\% \text{ of the class prefer sweets}$$

The percentages are statistics about food preferences of the class.

See data, per cent

straight angle

An angle of 180°.

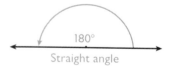

Straight angle

See angle

straight edge

An object that can be used to draw straight lines.

Example:

Blackboard ruler

straight line

See line, line segment

subset

A set within a set.

Examples:

(i) If each element of a set S (below) is also an element of a set T, then S is called a subset of T.

Set T = {Natural numbers to twenty-five}

Set S = {Square numbers to twenty-five}

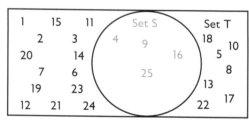

(ii) Set A = {all children in your class}

Set B = {all girls in your class}

Set B is a subset of set A, because all the elements in set B are also in set A.

See combination, set

substitution

(i) Something standing in place of another.

(ii) The replacement of a variable (a letter in a code message or a place holder in a number sentence) by a number.

Examples:

1. If a = 5 and b = 2, what is value of 2a + 2b?

$$2a + 2b = 2 \times 5 + 2 \times 2$$
$$= 10 + 4$$
$$= 14$$

2. In this secret code, numbers are substituted for letters.

A	B	C	D	E	F	G	...	2	1	4	7	5
1	2	3	4	5	6	7	...	B	A	D	G	E

See code, number sentence, place holder, variable

subtract

Take away.
Find the difference. Find the complement.

See difference, subtraction

subtraction

(i) Taking away (finding what is left).

Jessica had five pencils and gave three to Mario. How many pencils did Jessica keep?

 5 − 3 = ☐

5 − 3 = 2

Jessica kept 2 pencils.

(ii) Difference (comparison).

Remy has seven pencils and Robin has three pencils. How many more pencils has Remy than Robin?

 7 − 3 = ☐

7 − 3 = 4

Remy has 4 more pencils than Robin

(iii) Complementary addition (missing addend, counting on).

Rowan has three pencils, but needs seven. How many more must he get?

    3 + ☐4☐ = 7

3 + 4 = 7

Rowan must get 4 more pencils.

Subtraction may be represented on a number line:
Show on the number line:

$$5 - 3 = 2$$

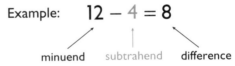

See complementary addition, difference, number line

subtrahend

A number which is to be subtracted from another number.

Example: **12 − 4 = 8**

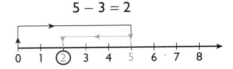

     minuend   subtrahend   difference

Four is the subtrahend.

See difference, minuend, subtract

sum

The answer to an addition problem. It is the total amount resulting from the addition of two or more numbers, quantities or magnitudes.

Example: **3 + 4 = 7**

     addends   sum

Seven is the sum.

See addend, addition

supplementary angles

Two angles which together make 180°.

Example:

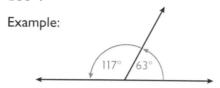

Angles 117° and 63° are supplementary.
Angle 117° is called the supplement of 63°.
Angle 63° is called the supplement of 117°.

See complementary angles, parallel lines

surface

(i)   The outside of something.

Example: The surface of the tennis ball is furry.

(ii) The top level of a liquid.

Example: Leaves float on the surface of a lake.

The surface of an object may be flat or curved.

Example:

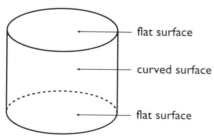

A cylinder has two flat surfaces and one curved.

See area, cylinder

surface area

The total area of the outside of a 3D shape.

Example:

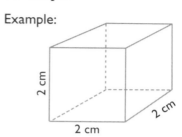

A cube with two centimetre sides has a surface area of
$6 \times (2 \times 2)$ cm^2 = 24 cm^2

See area, cube, surface

symbol

A letter, numeral or mark which represents something. We do not write a full stop after a symbol.

Examples:

1 2 3 + − × ÷
= ≠ > < ≈ % □
cm kg ha m^3 ∠
a b x^2 2x

See abbreviation, place holder, pronumeral, Useful Information page 149

symmetry

A shape has symmetry or is symmetrical when one half of the shape can fit exactly over the other half.

Shapes are called symmetrical if
they have one or more lines (axes)
of symmetry.

Examples:

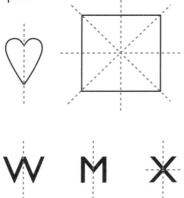

See asymmetry, line of symmetry,
rotational symmetry

Système
Internationale
d'Unités

See SI

t

Symbol for tonne.

table

(i) An arrangement of letters or numbers in rows or columns.

Example:

×	1	2	3	4	5	6
1	1	2	3	4	5	6
2	2	4	6	8	10	12
3	3	6	9	12	15	18
4	4	8	12	16	20	24
5	5	10	15	20	25	30
6	6	12	18	24	30	36

(ii) When multiplication facts are arranged in order, they are then called multiplication tables.

Example:

The tables of nine

$1 \times 9 = 9$ $6 \times 9 = 54$

$2 \times 9 = 18$ $7 \times 9 = 63$

$3 \times 9 = 27$ $8 \times 9 = 72$

$4 \times 9 = 36$ $9 \times 9 = 81$

$5 \times 9 = 45$ $10 \times 9 = 90$

See multiplication

take away

Remove, subtract. It is one of the ways of subtraction.

Example:
I had fifteen marbles and I lost seven. How many do I have now?

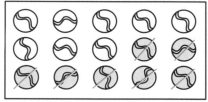

$15 - 7 = 8$ (take away seven from fifteen)

Answer: I have eight marbles now.

See subtraction

tally marks

A record of items made by placing a mark to represent each item. The marks are usually drawn in groups of five, with the fifth mark in each group crossing the other four, to make them easy to count.

Example: A tally of 13 items

//// //// ///

tangram

A Chinese puzzle made up of a square cut into seven pieces that can be rearranged to make many varied shapes.

Example:

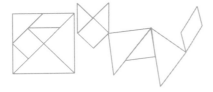

tape measure

A strip of tape or a thin metal marked with centimetres.

tare

Mass of wrapping in which goods are packed.

See gross mass

temperature

How hot or how cold something is. Temperature is measured in degrees Celsius (°C).

Examples:
(i) Water freezes (changes to ice) at 0°C.

(ii) Water boils at a 100°C.
(iii) Normal body temperature is 37°C.

See degree Celsius, thermometer

template

An instrument for drawing shapes. It may be one of two types:
(i) Cardboard or plastic pieces around which we draw.

Example:

(ii) A sheet of cardboard or firm plastic out of which shapes have been cut.

Example:

Template

term

(i) Each of two quantities in a ratio or a fraction: $\frac{3}{4}$ 1:7

(ii) Each of the quantities connected by + or − in an algebraic expression or equation.

$$3a - 3b \qquad y = x + 1$$

terminate

To come to an end, finish, not to go any further.

terminating decimal

A decimal fraction that is not recurring, that has 'an end'.

Example:

$\frac{1}{4} = 0.25$

$$\begin{array}{r} 0.25 \\ 4{\overline{)1.00}} \\ \underline{-8} \\ 20 \\ -20 \\ = \text{(end)} \end{array}$$

See recurring decimal

tessellation

A complete covering of a plane by one or more figures in a repeating pattern, with no overlapping of, or gaps between, the figures. Mosaic and pavement shapes tessellate.

Examples:

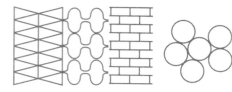

These shapes tessellate.   Circles do not tessellate.

Certain shapes will cover a surface completely: squares, equilateral triangles, hexagons, etc. These are said to 'tessellate'.

See circle, pattern, plane, square, triangle

tetragon

A plane shape with four sides and four angles.

See quadrilaterals

tetrahedron

A solid (polyhedron) with four faces. Also called triangular pyramid.
A regular tetrahedron is made of four congruent equilateral triangles and belongs to the group called platonic solids.

Examples:

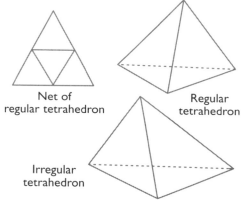

Net of regular tetrahedron

Regular tetrahedron

Irregular tetrahedron

See polyhedron, regular polyhedron

thermometer

An instrument for measuring temperature.

Example:

This thermometer shows a temperature of 100°C.

See degree Celsius, temperature

third

(i)   The ordinal number which comes after second and before fourth.

Example:

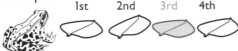

1st   2nd   3rd   4th

(ii)   One-third means one of three equal parts. Written as $\frac{1}{3}$.

Example:

$\frac{1}{3}$ has been coloured in $\boxed{\frac{1}{3}}$ $\frac{1}{3}$ $\frac{1}{3}$

See ordinal number

thousand

Ten hundreds, written as 1000.

See hundred

thousand separator

For easy reading, large numbers are divided into groups of three digits either side of the decimal point.

Example: 26 375 159.123 45

The correct separator is a narrow space between the groups of digits, as shown, not the comma that was used in the past.

three-dimensional
(3D)

When something has length, width and height, that is, three dimensions, then it is three-dimensional. Space figures (solids) are three-dimensional.

Example:

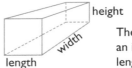

height

length   width

The sketch produces an illusion of depth, length and height.

See dimension, solid, sphere

time interval

The time that passes between two events.
Some units of time are:

second   s
minute   min
hour   h
day   d
week, month, year, decade, century, millenium

See unit of measurement

time line

A line on which intervals of time are recorded in chronological order.

Example:

1770	Captain Cook at Botany Bay
1788	Arrival of first fleet; convict settlement at Sydney Cove
1793	First free settlers arrive
1800	Hobart founded
1808	Rum rebellion
1810	Macquarie becomes Governor of NSW
1816	Sydney Hospital opened
1821	Governor Brisbane arrives
1828	First census: Population of NSW and Van Dieman's Land is 36 598
1835	John Batman arrives at Port Phillip Bay; Melbourne founded

See time interval

times

(Symbol: ×)

A word used for multiplication.

Examples:

When we multiply 3 × 5, we say
'three times five'.

Also, in 5(a + b), we say
'five times (a + b)'.

tonne

(Symbol: t)

A tonne is a metric unit for
measuring mass.

$$1 \text{ t} = 1000 \text{ kg}$$

Examples:

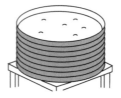

The mass of this empty utility is
1435 kilograms or 1.435 tonne.

This water tank contains 1000 litres of
water. The mass is 1000 kilograms or
one tonne.

See kilogram, litre, mass, metric system

topology

The part of mathematics that deals
with non-measurable properties of
things; of insides and outsides,
surfaces, shapes and connections.

Topology is concerned with relative
positions, not measurement.

Example:

Square ABCD can be distorted to look
like this:

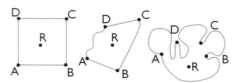

R always remains inside the figure.

Topology is sometimes called
'rubber-sheet geometry'.

See property

torus

A 3D shape, like a
doughnut or a tube.

total

(i)   Sum. When you add things or
values together, the answer is
the total.

Example:
$$10 + 20 + 25 = 55$$
                  ↑
               total

(ii) Whole.

Example:

The total area of the farm is
80 hectares.

See add, sum

transformation

(i)   The process by which the
shape, position or size of an
object is changed.

See enlarge, flip, projection, reduce,
reflection, rotation, translation

(ii) The process by which the form of an expression is changed.

Examples: $\frac{1}{2} = 0.5 = 50\%$

The formula for finding the area:
$A = \ell \times w$, can be transformed into:
$$\ell = \frac{A}{w}$$

(iii) The process by which a set of numbers (or objects) is associated in one-to-one or many-to-one correspondence with another set of numbers (or objects).

See many-to-one correspondence, one-to-one correspondence

translation

When a shape is moved along a straight line without being flipped, rotated or reflected, we say it has been translated.

Example:

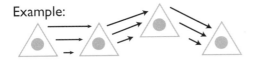

See flip, reflection, rotation, slide, turn

transversal

A straight line crossing two or more lines.

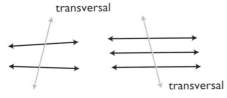

See line, parallel lines

trapezium

A four-sided figure (quadrilateral) with one pair of sides parallel and the other pair not parallel.

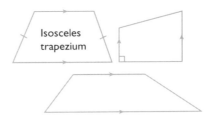

When the two sides that are not parallel are equal, then the trapezium is isosceles.

See isosceles triangle, parallel, quadrilateral

trapezoid

A quadrilateral with no parallel sides.

traversable

A curve or route is traversable if it can be traced without lifting the pencil or going over any part of the curve more than once.

Examples:

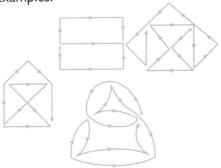

These routes are traversable.

treble

Make three times bigger or multiply by three.

See multiplication

triangle

A polygon with three sides and three angles. We can classify triangles by sides or by angles.

(i) By sides

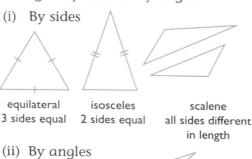

equilateral	isosceles	scalene
3 sides equal	2 sides equal	all sides different in length

(ii) By angles

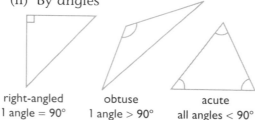

right-angled	obtuse	acute
1 angle = 90°	1 angle > 90°	all angles < 90°

The sum of angles inside a triangle is always 180°.

See equilateral triangle, isosceles triangle, plane shape, right-angled triangle, scalene triangle, sum

triangle number

(triangular number)

A number that can be represented by dots in the shape of a triangle.

Examples:

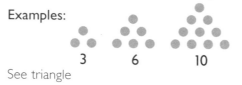

3   6   10

See triangle

trillion

A trillion is a million millions, that is, 1 000 000 000 000, or 10^{12}. It used to be a thousand billions, or 10^{18}.

See Large numbers on page 154

true sentence

A sentence about numbers that is true or correct.

Examples:

$3 \times 2 = 2 \times 3$ is a true sentence.

$6 \neq 5$ is a true sentence.

The open sentence $2 + \square = 9$ becomes true, if $\square$ is replaced by 7. If $\square$ is replaced by any other number, then it will become a false sentence.

See false sentence, number sentence, open sentence

trundle wheel

A wheel, usually one metre in circumference, used for measuring distance. The wheel often gives a click sound at each revolution (one metre), so the number of metres can be counted.

See circumference, metre

turn

Move. Change position. Rotate.

See rotation

twelve-hour time

A period of one day (twenty-four hours) divided into two halves of twelve hours each.
Twelve-hour time should include a.m. and p.m.

Example:

This clock shows
either 7:45 a.m.
or 7:45 p.m.

See a.m., p.m., twenty-four hour time

twenty-four hour time

A period of one day divided into twenty-four hourly divisions, to prevent errors between a.m. and p.m. times.

Example:

A 24-hour clock

12-hour time	24-hour time
1 a.m.	0100 one hundred hours
10 a.m.	1000 ten hundred hours
1 p.m.	1300 thirteen hundred hours
3:40 p.m.	1540 fifteen-forty hours

See a.m., p.m., twelve-hour time

twice

Two times, or double.

Example:
Twice six is $2 \times 6 = 12$

two-dimensional
(2D)

When something has length and width, then it has two dimensions and is two-dimensional. Plane shapes and surfaces have two dimensions.

Examples:

Plane regions have two dimensions.

See dimension, length, plane shape, region, surface, width

unequal

(Symbol: $\neq$)

Not equal.

Example:

$$3 \neq 4$$

Read as:
'Three is not equal to four'.

See inequality, not equal

union

Combining two or more things.

unit

Unit is another name for one. The unit column in our number system refers to the first column to the left of the decimal point. In 425.0, the unit digit is 5.

425.0

— tenths column
— units column
— tens column
— hundreds column

See metric system, unit of measurement

unitary method

A simple way of solving problems, by working out the value of one unit.

Example:

Five kilograms of grapes cost $14.50. How much for three kilograms?

$$5 \text{ kg} = \$14.50$$
$$1 \text{ kg} = \frac{\$14.50}{5} = \$2.90$$
$$3 \text{ kg} = \$2.90 \times 3 = \$8.70$$

unit, basic

Units, including those for mass, length and time, form the basis for a system of measurement.

Example:

The metre, the kilogram and the second are base units of the metric system (SI).

See metric relationships on page 154, metric system, unit of measurement

unit of measurement

A standard unit such as a kilometre, gram, minute, litre, etc.

See standard

unit square

A square with sides of length equal to one unit of length or distance.

Example:
A square with sides one metre long has an area of one square metre (1 m^2).

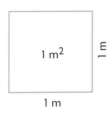

See distance, unit of measurement

unknown value

In number sentences, algebraic expressions or equations, the unknown values are represented by pronumerals or variables.

Examples:

$2\boxed{} = 10$
↑
unknown value

$x - 7 \geq 5$
↑
unknown value

$2a - 2b$
↘ ↗
unknown values

See number sentence, pronumeral, variable

unlike terms

Terms that are not like.

Examples:

$2a + 3b$
↘ ↗
unlike terms

$2a + a$
↘ ↗
like terms

Unlike terms cannot be combined or simplified by adding or subtracting.

See like terms

V

Symbol for volume.

value

(i) When an expression is simplified, the result is the value of the expression.

Example:
$$\frac{3+5}{2} \times 7$$
$$= \frac{8}{2} \times 7$$
$$= 4 \times 7$$
$$= 28$$
28 is the value of $\frac{3+5}{2} \times 7$

(ii) When solving equations, we evaluate them.

Example:

Find the value of $\frac{x+5}{2}$, if $x = 10$.

Answer : $\frac{10+5}{2} = 7.5$

7.5 is the value.

(iii) The amount of money something is worth.

Example:

A walkman costs $78. Its value is $78.

See equation, evaluate, place value, substitute

vanishing point

In perspective, the point or points at which all parallel lines appear to meet.

vanishing point

See perspective

variable

(i) A symbol or letter representing an unknown member of a set. In algebraic expressions, a variable stands for a value. Sometimes it is called an unknown.

Example:
In $x^2 + 3x + 2 = 0$, x is the variable.

(ii) The same variable may have different values under different conditions.

Example:

$$x + 3 = 5 \qquad x = 2$$
$$x - 1 = 10 \qquad x = 11$$

(iii) A mathematical sentence that has at least one variable is called an open sentence.

Example:

$x + 3 = 7$ is true only when $x = 4$.

The number 4 is called the solution of $x + 3 = 7$.

If x is replaced by any other number, the sentence will become not true (false).

See algebra, algebraic expression, number sentence, open sentence, place holder, pronumeral, symbol

Venn diagram

A diagram used to represent sets and relationships between sets.

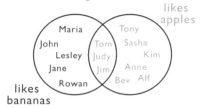

See diagram, set

vertex

(Plural: vertices)

Top, the highest part or point. A point where two or more adjacent lines meet to form an angle or a corner.

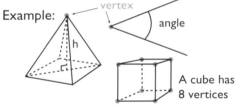

A cube has 8 vertices

In plane or solid figures, the vertex is the point opposite the base.

See apex, arm of an angle

vertical

A vertical line is perpendicular (at right angles) to the horizon.

Examples:

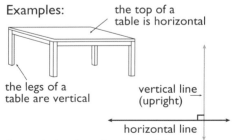

the top of a table is horizontal

the legs of a table are vertical

vertical line (upright)

horizontal line

See axis, horizon, horizontal line, perpendicular, right angle

vertically opposite angles

When two lines intersect, they make four angles at the vertex. The angles opposite each other are equal in size and are called vertically opposite angles.

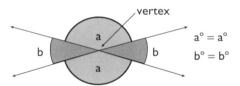

vertex

$a° = a°$
$b° = b°$

See complementary angles, parallel lines, supplementary angles, vertex

volume

The amount of space inside a container, or the actual amount of material in the container.

Example:
The volume of this object is 36 cubic units.

Some units of volume are:

For the volume of solids:
cubic centimetre cm^3
cubic metre m^3

For the volume of liquids:
millilitre   mL
litre   L
kilolitre   kL
megalitre   ML

See capacity, cubic centimetre, cubic metre, cubic unit, metric relationships on page 151, solid

vulgar fraction

See simple fraction

Astronaut in space:
His mass is still 75 kg.
But he is weightless.

week

A period of time: seven days. There are fifty-two weeks in a year.

See days of the week

weight

The pull of gravity on an object. The true meaning of the term 'weight' is a complicated physics problem. The weight of an object changes with the change of the gravitational pull. The mass of an object (the amount of matter the object is made of) remains constant.

Example:

Astronauts become weightless in space but the mass of their bodies does not change.

Astronaut on Earth:
His mass = 75 kg
His weight ≈ 75 kg

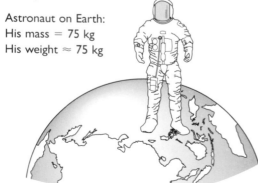

People often speak incorrectly of weight when they really mean mass.

See mass

whole numbers

Zero together with all counting numbers.

{0, 1, 2, 3, 4, 5, 6, 7, 8,...}

See counting number, zero

width

The measurement from side to side. Also called breadth.

Example:

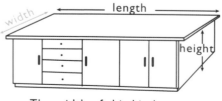

The width of this kitchen bench is 70 cm

x-axis y-axis

See coordinates

yard

The old imperial measure of length.

$$1 \text{ yard} = 36 \text{ inches} \approx 90 \text{ cm}$$

year

The period of time it takes the Earth to make one complete revolution around the Sun: 365 days, 5 hours and 48 $\frac{3}{4}$ minutes. The extra hours, minutes and seconds are put together into an extra day every four years to form a 'leap year'.

See day, leap year, revolution

zero

(Symbol: 0, Ø)

The numeral 0 (nought). Nothing.
Rules for working with zero:
1 A number + 0 = same number
$$5 + 0 = 5$$
2 A number − 0 = same number
$$7 - 0 = 7$$

3 A number × 0 = 0
$$6 \times 0 = 0$$
4 0 ÷ any number = 0
$$0 \div 10 = 0$$
5 A number ÷ 0 has no answer
$$3 \div 0 = \text{can't do}$$

The digit zero is used as a place holder in numerals.

Example:
In the number sixty, 0 is a place holder for units to show that the 6 means six tens and there are no single units.

Note: These words all mean zero: nil, nought, none, nix, null, oh, void, empty set, zilch, duck (in cricket), love (in tennis).

See digit, place holder

zero power

When working with indices, any number raised to the power zero always equals one. It happens because when we divide indices, we subtract the indexes and get zero.

$$2^0 = 1 \qquad 376^0 = 1 \qquad x^0 = 1$$

Example:
Find the value of:

$$5^2 \div 5^2 \qquad\qquad 5^2 \div 5^2$$
$$= 5 \times 5 \div 5 \times 5 \qquad = 5^{(2-2)}$$
$$= 25 \div 25 \qquad\qquad = 5^0$$
$$= 1 \qquad\qquad = 1$$

See index, index laws, power

Useful Information

units of measurement

length

10 millimetres (mm) = 1 centimetre (cm)
100 centimetres (cm) = 1 metre (m)
1000 millimetres (mm) = 1 metre (m)
1000 metres (m) = 1 kilometre (km)

area

100 square millimetres (mm^2)
= 1 square centimetre (cm^2)

10 000 square centimetres (cm^2)
= 1 square metre (m^2)

10 000 square metres (m^2)
= 1 hectare (ha)

100 hectares (ha) = 1 square kilometre (km^2)
= 1 000 000 square metres (m^2)

mass

1000 milligrams (mg) = 1 gram (g)
1000 grams (g) = 1 kilogram (kg)
1000 kilograms (kg) = 1 tonne (t)

liquid volume

1000 millilitres (mL) = 1 litre (L)
1 mL (for liquids) = 1 cm^3 (for solids)
1000 litres (L) = 1 kilolitre (kL)
1 kL (for liquids) = 1 m^3 (for solids)

solids volume

1 cubic centimetre (cm^3)
1 cubic metre (m^3)

time

60 seconds (s)   = 1 minute (min)
60 minutes (min) = 1 hour (h)
24 hours (h)   = 1 day (d)
7 days   = 1 week
365 days   = 1 year
366 days   = 1 leap year
12 months   = 1 year
10 years   = 1 decade
100 years   = 1 century
1000 years   = 1 millenium

symbols

m   metre
g   gram
L   litre
t   tonne
m^2 square metre
m^3 cubic metre
ha   hectare
°C   degree Celsius

Remember: These are the correct symbols:

mm   cm   m   km
mL   L   kL
mg   g   kg   t
mm^2 cm^2 m^2 ha   km^2
cm^3 m^3
s   min   h   d

angle measure

1 degree (1°)   = 60 minutes (60′)
1 minute (1′)   = 60 seconds (60″)
1 right angle   = 90 degrees (90°)
1 straight angle = 180 degrees (180°)
1 revolution   = 360 degrees (360°)

a list of symbols

Symbol	Meaning	Example
$+$	addition sign, add, plus	$2 + 1 = 3$
$-$	subtraction sign, subtract, take away, minus	$7 - 6 = 1$
$\times$	multiplication sign, multiply by, times	$3 \times 3 = 9$
$\div\ )\overline{}$	division sign, divide by	$9 \div 2 = 4.5$
$=$	is equal to, equals	$2 + 2 = 1 + 3$
$\neq$	is not equal to	$2 \neq 5$
$\doteqdot \approx \cong$	is approximately equal to	$302 \approx 300$
$\leq$	is less than or equal to	$x \leq 12$
$\geq$	is greater than or equal to	$5 \geq y$
$>$	is greater than	$7 > 6.9$
$<$	is less than	$2 < 4$
$\nless$	is not less than	$6 \nless 5$
$\ngtr$	is not greater than	$3.3 \ngtr 3.4$
c	cent(s)	50c
$\$$	dollar(s)	$\$1.20$
.	decimal point (on the line)	5.24
%	per cent, out of 100	50%
$^\circ$	degree Celsius, degree (angle measure)	$^\circ$C $\quad 35^\circ$C $\quad 90^\circ$
$'$	minutes (angle measure)	$5^\circ 35'$
' foot	feet (imperial system)	$1' \approx 30$ cm
$''$	seconds (angle measure)	$12^\circ 05' 24''$
" inch	inches (imperial system)	$12'' = 1'$
$\angle \wedge$	angle	$\angle$AOB $\quad$ B$\widehat{O}$C
$\triangle$	triangle	$\triangle$ ABC
$\parallel$	parallel lines, is parallel to	AB $\parallel$ CD
$\not\equiv$ $\dagger\dagger$	line segments of the same length	
$\llcorner$	right angle, 90°	
$\perp$	is perpendicular to, at 90°	$h \perp b$
$\sqrt{}$	square root	$\sqrt{4} = \pm 2$
$\sqrt[3]{}$	cube root	$\sqrt[3]{27} = 3$
π	pi, $\pi \doteqdot 3.14$	$C = 2\pi r$
$\equiv \cong$	is congruent to	$\triangle$ ABC $\equiv \triangle$ DEF

Roman numerals

	Thousands	Hundreds	Tens	Units
1	M	C	X	I
2	MM	CC	XX	II
3	MMM	CCC	XXX	III
4		CD	XL	IV
5		D	L	V
6		DC	LX	VI
7		DCC	LXX	VII
8		DCCC	LXXX	VIII
9		CM	XC	IX

EXAMPLE:　1　9　9　9 = MCMXCIX

M CM XC IX

parts of a circle

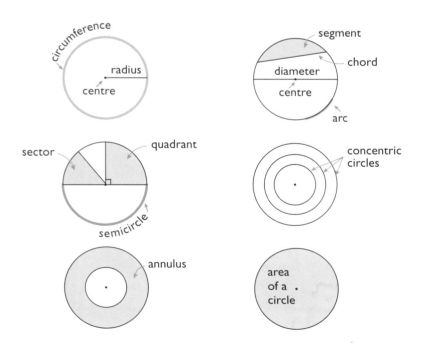

metric relationships

Length	Area	Volume	Capacity

Length	Area	Volume	Capacity
1 cm	1 cm^2	1 cm^3	1 mL
10 mm	100 mm^2	1000 mm^3	One 1 cm cube (cubic centimetre) has a capacity of 1 millilitre.

 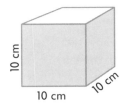 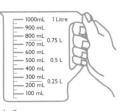

10 cm	100 cm^2	1000 cm^3	1 L
100 mm	10 000 mm^2	1 000 000 mm^3	One 10 cm cube (1000 cm^3) has a capacity of 1 litre.

 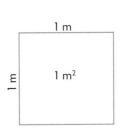  

1 m	1 m^2	1 m^3	1 kL
100 cm	10 000 cm^2	1 000 000 cm^3	One cubic metre has a capacity of 1 kilolitre. These 5 drums each hold 1 kilolitre.

formulae

Plane shapes	Diagram	Area	Perimeter
circle		$A = \pi r^2$	$C = 2\pi r = \pi d$
square		$A = a^2$	$P = 4a$
rectangle		$A = ab$	$P = 2(a + b)$
kite		$A = \dfrac{ab}{2}$	
trapezium		$A = \dfrac{a + b}{2} \times h$	$P = a + b + c + d$
parallelogram		$A = ah$	$P = 2(a + b)$
rhombus		$A = ah$	$P = 4a$
triangle		$A = \dfrac{1}{2}bh$	$P = a + b + c$

more formulae

Solids	Diagram	Volume	Surface area
cube		$V = a^3$	$S = 6a^2$
cuboid		$V = \ell wh$	$S = 2(\ell w + h\ell + hw)$
pyramid		$V = \frac{1}{3} \text{base} \times h$	$S = \text{area of base} + 4 \times \text{Area of } \triangle$
cylinder		$V = \pi r^2 h$	$S = 2 \times \pi r^2 + 2\pi rh$ $= 2\pi r\,(r + h)$
cone		$V = \frac{1}{3}\pi r^2 h$	
sphere	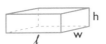	$V = \frac{4}{3}\pi r^3$	$S = 4\pi r^2$
Pythagoras' theorem		$c^2 = a^2 + b^2$ $a = \sqrt{c^2 - b^2}$ $b = \sqrt{c^2 - a^2}$ $c = \sqrt{a^2 + b^2}$	

large numbers

		Australia, USA	UK
million	1000×1000	10^6	10^6
billion	1000 millions	10^9	10^{12} (million millions)
trillion	1000 billions	10^{12}	10^{18} (million billions)
quadrillion	million billions	10^{15}	10^{24} (billion billions)

letters used in mathematics

In sets:

I	integers
N	natural numbers
Q	rational numbers
R	real numbers
W	whole numbers

In geometry:

a, b, c, d, ...	sides of polygons
	lengths of intervals
	names of lines
A, B, C, D, ...	points, vertices
A	area of polygons
b	base of polygons
C	circumference of a circle
d	diameter of a circle
h	height
l, l	length
O	origin, centre of a circle
P	perimeter
r	radius of a circle
s	side
S, SA	surface area
V	volume of solids
w	width

decimal system prefixes

Prefix	Symbol	Value	Value in words	Example	Meaning
pico	p	10^{-12}	one trillionth of	1 pF	picofarad
nano	n	10^{-9}	one thousand millionth of	1 ns	nanosecond
micro	μ	10^{-6}	one millionth of	1 μs	microsecond
milli	m	10^{-3}	one thousandth of	1 mg	milligram
centi	c	10^{-2}	one hundredth of	1 cm	centimetre
deci	d	10^{-1}	one tenth of	1 dB	decibel
			unit		
deca	d, D	10^{1}	10 times	not commonly used in Australia	
hecto	h	10^{2}	100 times	1 hL	hectolitre
kilo	k	10^{3}	1000 times	1 kg	kilogram
mega	M	10^{6}	1 million times	1 ML	megalitre
giga	G	10^{9}	1 thousand million times	1 GB	gigabyte

numerical prefixes

Prefix	Meaning	Example
mono	1	monorail
bi	2	bicycle, binary
tri	3	tricycle, triangle
tetra	4	tetrahedron, tetrapack
quad	4	quadrilateral, quads
penta, quin	5	pentagon
hexa	6	hexagon
hepta, septi	7	heptagon
octa	8	octagon
nona, nov	9	nonagon
deca	10	decagon, decahedron
undeca	11	undecagon
dodeca	12	dodecagon, dodecahedron
icosa	20	icosahedron
hect	100	hectare
kilo	1000	kilogram
mega	1 000 000	megalitre, megawatt
giga	1 000 million	gigabyte

other prefixes

Prefix	Meaning	Example
anti	opposite, against	anti-clockwise
circum	around	circumference
co	together	cointerior, coordinate
geo	earth	geometry
hemi	half	hemisphere
macro	very big	macrocosmos
micro	very small	microbe
multi	many, much	multibase blocks
peri	around	perimeter
poly	many	polygon
semi	half	semicircle
sub	below, under	subset
trans	across, beyond, over	transversal
uni	one, having one	unit

the multiplication square

×	1	2	3	4	5	6	7	8	9	10
1	1	2	3	4	5	6	7	8	9	10
2	2	4	6	8	10	12	14	16	18	20
3	3	6	9	12	15	18	21	24	27	30
4	4	8	12	16	20	24	28	32	36	40
5	5	10	15	20	25	30	35	40	45	50
6	6	12	18	24	30	36	42	48	54	60
7	7	14	21	28	35	42	49	56	63	70
8	8	16	24	32	40	48	56	64	72	80
9	9	18	27	36	45	54	63	72	81	90
10	10	20	30	40	50	60	70	80	90	100

Greek alphabet

The letters of the Greek alphabet are used as symbols for angles, mathematical operations, etc.

Examples:

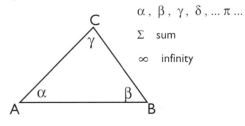

α, β, γ, δ, ... π ...

Σ sum

∞ infinity

Capital	Lower case	Handwritten	Pronunciation
A	α	α	alpha
B	β	β	beta .
Γ	γ	γ	gamma
Δ	δ	δ	delta
E	ϵ	ε	epsilon
Z	ζ	ζ	zeta
H	η	η	eta
Θ	θ	θ	theta
I	ι	ι	iota
K	κ	κ	kappa
Λ	λ	λ	lambda
M	μ	μ	mu
N	ν	ν	nu
Ξ	ξ	ξ	xi
O	o	o	omicron
Π	π	π	pi
P	ρ	ρ	rho
Σ	σ	σ	sigma
T	τ	τ	tau
Υ	υ	u	upsilon
Φ	ϕ	φ	phi
X	χ	x	chi
Ψ	ψ	ψ	psi
Ω	ω	ω	omega